BODY LANGUAGE

An Illustrated Introduction for Teachers

Patrick W. Miller, Ph.D.

Patrick W. Miller and Associates — Munster, Indiana — www.pwmilleronline.com

Body Language: An Illustrated Introduction for Teachers

 Observations expressed in this book are from a "Western" or American perspective. For more information, visit www.pwmilleronline.com.

About the Author

Patrick W. Miller, Ph.D. has been writing about body language for more than 25 years. His monograph *Nonverbal Communication: What Research Says to the Teacher* was on the National Education Association's best seller list for 15 years. Miller annually speaks to thousands of educators across the nation on body language. His animated presentation style brings home many real-life experiences that directly relate to classroom and family situations.

Acknowledgments

The author wishes to thank Jean Ellen Miller for assistance in preparing the manuscript, Alex Patrick Miller for maintaining the computers, Tatum Bree Hindman for Web site programming, and Joy Olivia Miller for the book's layout. A special thanks also goes to Laura Burke, Marshal Chaifetz, Claudia LeBeau, and Patrick Owens for their helpful suggestions and comments during the editing process.

Library of Congress Control Number 2004099878

ISBN 0967327989

TABLE OF CONTENTS

INTRODUCTION

People are always communicating. Communication—an ongoing process of sending and receiving messages—enables us to share knowledge, express attitudes, and demonstrate skills. Explicit and implicit communication occurs whenever teachers and students interact. Successful teaching depends on effective communication in the classroom.

> **"The mediocre teacher tells. The good teacher explains. The superior teacher demonstrates. The great teacher inspires."**
>
> William Arthur Ward

Communication has multiple dimensions—verbal and nonverbal being the most interactive forms. Educators, psychologists, anthropologists, and sociologists define body language or nonverbal communication as communication without words. It includes overt behaviors such as facial expressions, eye contact, touching, and tone of voice, as well as less obvious messages communicated through dress, posture, and spatial distance. The most effective and persuasive communication occurs

Educators, psychologists, anthropologists, and sociologists define nonverbal communication as communication without words.

True feelings are vividly expressed through nonverbal actions.

"You never get a second chance to make a first impression."

Will Rogers

"It takes five hundred small details to add up to one favorable impression."

Cary Grant

"Of those who say nothing, few are silent."

Thomas Neill

when verbal and nonverbal messages are in sync, creating communication synergy.

Social psychologists suggest that we begin to form impressions within seconds of meeting someone for the first time. During this short period, judgments are made about one's character, personality, intelligence, temperament, working habits, and suitability as a friend. These conclusions—although often based on little information—form impressions that are seldom changed (Gladwell, 2005).

Teachers and students constantly send messages. Consciously and unconsciously, they send and receive nonverbal cues several hundred times a day.

A recent study asked college students to rate professors' personality traits based on a 10-second recording of their teaching. Findings indicated that these ratings were uncannily similar to those made by students who completed an entire semester with the same professors. The study clearly demonstrated that exposure to even short periods of nonverbal behavior communicates a great deal about individuals (Ambady, 2004).

People make judgments the moment they see you based on your nonverbal communication. Your body communicates confidence—or lack of it—long before you utter your first words. You are your best or worst visual aid. Even when people do not move, they transmit messages by physique, gender, and ethnicity. Everything communicates, including material objects, physical space, and time systems.

Although verbal output can be turned off, nonverbal communication cannot. Even silence speaks.

Verbal communication permits instant feedback; nonverbal acts do not. Herein lies the difficulty. We can hear ourselves speak and make

"I speak two languages, body and English."

Mae West

"Say what you mean and mean what you say."

George S. Patton

Verbal communication permits instant feedback; nonverbal acts do not.

Children first learn nonverbal expressions by watching and imitating.

"Children have never been very good at listening to their elders, but they have never failed to imitate them."

James Baldwin

"Don't worry that children never listen to you; worry that they are always watching you."

Robert Fulghum

corrections. However, we cannot see our own nonverbal messages, so we must rely on instinct and understanding of nonverbal communication as well as feedback from others.

Nonverbal communication is learned shortly after birth, then practiced and refined throughout a person's lifetime. Even before language emerges, infant behaviors communicate. Children first learn nonverbal expressions by watching and imitating, much as they learn verbal skills. Young children know far more than they can verbalize and are generally more adept at reading nonverbal cues than adults because of their limited verbal skills and their recent reliance on nonverbal messages to communicate. At approximately one year of age, children use distance, eye contact, gestures, touch, vocal intonation patterns, and smiling to communicate with others. As children develop verbal skills, nonverbal channels of communication do not cease to exist. Rather, the nonverbal messages become intertwined in the total communication process. These lessons are fundamental because emotions may be communicated through nonverbal channels.

We use nonverbal communication for the following reasons:

Words have limitations. Through the use of words, we are able to communicate far better than animals; however, there are still numerous areas where nonverbal communication is more effective. For example, most people find it difficult to explain the shape of something or to give directions without using hand gestures or head nods. Similarly, personality characteristics are expressed nonverbally, enabling others to form clear impressions, which they ultimately use to direct their responses.

Nonverbal signals are powerful. Because nonverbal cues primarily express inner feelings, they generally evoke immediate action or response. Basically, verbal messages deal with the outside world; therefore, the information must first be considered and its implications explored. Action is immediate only when highly trained individuals receive commands or orders.

Teachers should record themselves teaching a class to observe and correct nonverbal actions.

Reading body language is a matter of paying attention.

"The most important things are the hardest things to say. They are the things you get ashamed of because words diminish your feelings—words shrink things that seem limitless when they are in your head to no more than living size when they are brought out."

Stephen King

Body language is more authentic than spoken words.

Nonverbal messages are likely to be more genuine. Except for facial expressions and tone of voice, nonverbal behaviors cannot be controlled as easily as spoken words. Moreover, only by modifying the emotional state, which is far more difficult than modifying the body message, can one control signals such as pupil dilation and perspiration.

Nonverbal signals can express feelings too disturbing to state. Social etiquette limits what can be said, but nonverbal cues can communicate thoughts. In interpersonal relationships, it is quite rude to say "I don't like you" or "I'm better than you" to someone, but both sentiments can be expressed nonverbally. Thus, if people have not verbalized their feelings, they can conveniently change their minds freely without having committed themselves.

A separate communication channel is necessary to help send complex messages. In addition to expressing feelings and other personal information, nonverbal actions greatly enhance verbal communication. Vocal intonation alone tells when a speaker has finished a sentence, what is most important, and even when the speech has ended. A speaker can add enormously to the complexity of the verbal message through the use of simple nonverbal signals.

Body language indicates our emotions, regardless of whether we speak or keep silent.

"The most important thing in communication is to hear what isn't being said."

Peter F. Drucker

RESEARCH

Nonverbal behaviors can be amazingly subtle or very explicit; they may either support or contradict the verbal message being transmitted. Some research findings suggest that two-thirds of our communication is nonverbal. Other experts have suggested that only seven percent of a message is sent through words, with the remaining 93 percent sent through facial expressions (55 percent) and vocal intonation (38 percent) (Mehrabian, 1968). Words are accented and punctuated by body movements and gestures, while the face shows a myriad of expressions. Thus, nonverbal and verbal messages are intertwined as inseparable parts of human communication.

It is important to be aware of the dominance of nonverbal messages. Whenever incongruity exists between verbal and nonverbal messages, the nonverbal will win hands down. Also, the validity and reliability of verbal messages is checked by nonverbal actions. If a discrepancy exists, the nonverbal will dictate.

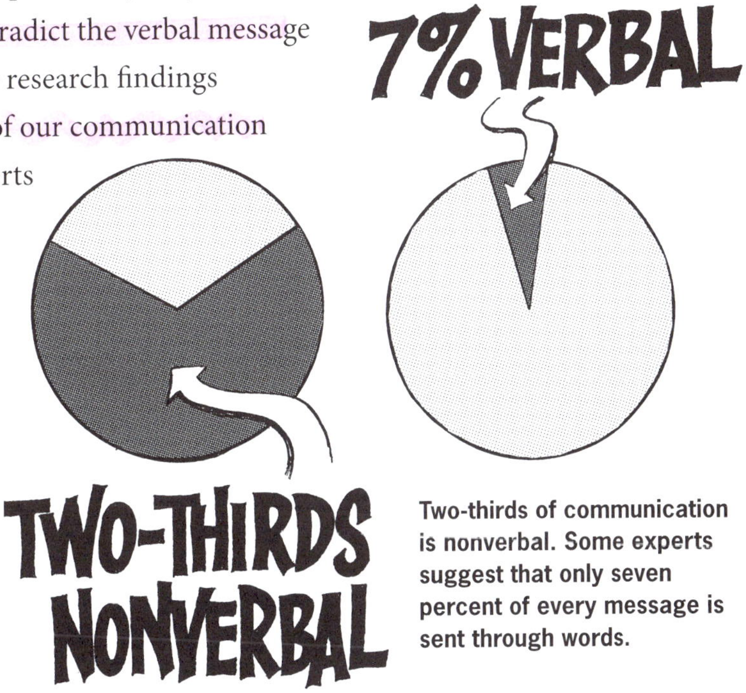

7% VERBAL

TWO-THIRDS NONVERBAL

Two-thirds of communication is nonverbal. Some experts suggest that only seven percent of every message is sent through words.

"He that has eyes to see and ears to hear may convince himself that no mortal can keep a secret. If his lips are silent, he chatters with his fingertips; betrayal oozes out of him at every pore."

Sigmund Freud

"Wise men read very sharply all your private history in your look and gait and behavior. The whole economy of nature is bent on expression. The telltale body is all tongues. Men are like Geneva watches with crystal faces which express the whole movement."

Ralph Waldo Emerson

Teachers should be aware of nonverbal communication in the classroom for two basic reasons: to become better receivers of all students' messages, and to gain the ability to send positive signals that reinforce students' learning while simultaneously becoming more skilled at avoiding negative signals that stifle their learning.

Numerous professionals employ a multitude of nonverbal behaviors to convey messages. Advertisers are aware of the integral part nonverbal communication plays in television commercials. Most creative thoughts of engineers and graphic designers are expressed nonverbally through drawings. Teachers also have a repertoire of nonverbal behaviors that affect students, both positively and negatively. Research suggests that students' nonverbal expressions serve as an important source in the formation of a teacher's impressions, attitudes, beliefs, and reciprocal behavioral expressions. Being a good message receiver

Communication requires at least two people—a sender and a receiver.

A large number of professionals—such as television directors, teachers, graphic designers, actors, football referees, and symphony conductors—employ a multitude of nonverbal behaviors in a systematic manner to convey messages.

requires more than just listening to words. Much is communicated by nonverbal means, such as feelings and values. Thus, to be a good receiver of student messages, a teacher must be attuned to many of these subtle nonverbal cues.

Just as it is important to be good receivers, it is important to develop nonverbal "sending" skills. Imagine for a moment how difficult it would be to teach a course by telephone or e-mail. Without the

"You can have brilliant ideas, but if you can't get them across, your ideas won't get you anywhere."

Lee Iacocca

Teachers and students send and receive nonverbal cues daily.

Teaching by telephone or e-mail would be difficult because of the absence of the nonverbal dialogue.

help of the nonverbal dialogue that goes on in the classroom, teachers would not be able to assess their teaching methods and strategies as they ordinarily do. For example, students use smiles, frowns, nodding heads, and other not-so-obvious cues to tell teachers to slow down, speed up, or in some other way modify the delivery of instructional material.

Not only are teachers often unaware of students' nonverbal behaviors, but they are also oblivious to the nonverbal messages they relay to students. Teachers express enthusiasm, warmth, assertiveness, confidence, or displeasure through their facial expressions, vocal intonation, gestures, and use of space. Teachers reinforce or modify student behavior by their use of smiles, winks, scowls, and the "evil eye." In addition, there are many other less common methods of nonverbal communication. Touch, for example, is often overlooked as a means of transmitting a message.

Telephone calls, e-mails, and faxes are forms of communication that exclude most nonverbal signals.

When teachers exhibit verbal messages that conflict with nonverbal messages, students become confused. This confusion often affects their attitudes and learning. Evidence from clinical and neurosurgical research indicates that the left hemisphere of the brain is involved primarily in verbal and other analytical functions, while the right hemisphere is responsible for spatial and nonverbal processes. If conflicting messages are communicated to these two hemispheric modes, each hemisphere emphasizes only one of the messages and omits information from the other.

Without words, teachers communicate their feelings, expectations, and many other messages they would never verbally admit. Students know when something bothers their teacher, whom their teacher likes or dislikes, as well as a surprising amount of other information that teachers think they keep to themselves.

Verbal and nonverbal messages should match when communicating with students.

Pygmalion in the Classroom, considered one of the most intriguing and controversial publications in the history of educational research, supports the premise that teacher expectations (manifested nonverbally) can foster academic achievement. This classic study involved administering a relatively unknown IQ test to elementary school children in a low socioeconomic area.

"What you do speaks so loudly that I cannot hear what you say."

Ralph Waldo Emerson

After testing, prospective teachers received a list of students' names identified as high scorers. In

Teachers convey nonverbal messages through facial expressions, body movements and gestures, touch, spatial relationships, and dress.

reality, these students were chosen at random, not as a consequence of the test results. The teachers were told to expect a great increase in intellectual performance from them. Ironically, at the end of the school year, these students did make sharp increases on IQ test scores.

Obviously, the teachers did not tell the students they expected higher performances, but they may have conveyed such messages nonverbally through facial expressions, gestures, touch, and spatial relationships. These subtle nonverbal expectancy behaviors may have been all the students needed to change their self-image, motivation, or achievement (Rosenthal & Jacobsen, 1968).

"High expectations are the key to everything."

Sam Walton

"We tend to live up to our expectations."

Earl Nightingale

The eponymous effect is also mentioned in George Bernard Shaw's play *Pygmalion,* adapted for the screen as *My Fair Lady,* in which Professor Henry Higgins insists he can turn a flower girl into a duchess. His success is emphasized by Eliza Doolittle's reply to Higgins' friend Colonel Pickering: "...the difference between a lady and a flower girl is not how she behaves, but how she's treated. I shall always be a flower girl to Professor Higgins, because he always treats me as a flower girl, and always will; but, I know I can be a lady to you because you always treat me as a lady, and always will."

The play *Pygmalion* and the movie *My Fair Lady* emphasize the reality of expectations.

In another study, volunteers recruited to tutor elementary school students were told the experiment involved testing the psychological effects of lighting, and that they were to present a five-minute lesson on home and family safety. The tutors were also read a statement about the students' abilities, classifying them as "bright," "average," or "below average." After this brief explanation, each tutor was individually led into a room to present the lesson to the elementary school child. In fact, the study

"If everybody thought before they spoke, the silence would be deafening."

George Barzan

did not measure the effects of lighting (which was only necessary to record the lesson), but rather the effect of the tutors' expectancies (conveying preconceived notions about intelligence and motivation) on nonverbal behaviors.

After the recordings were evaluated by trained raters, it was concluded that tutors in the microteaching lesson exhibited patterns of nonverbal behavior toward students classified as "bright" that were different from those exhibited toward students classified as "average" or "below average." The nonverbal behaviors displayed to "bright" students included touching, proximity, forward body lean, eye contact, more gestures, approving head nods, and positive facial expressions. Such findings point out the need for teachers to be more conscious about judging students before they have a chance to prove (or improve) themselves. Despite efforts to be unbiased, fair, and just, teachers may have preconceived opinions about certain students, gained either from colleagues or hearsay.

Teachers should be aware of nonverbal messages sent to students.

Teacher expectations can be influenced by a student's physical appearance.

PHYSICAL ATTRACTIVENESS

Physical appearance can also influence teacher expectations. One study asked teachers to evaluate students' intellectual potential based on report card grades, verbal descriptions, and pictures of an attractive or an unattractive student.

Even though the demographic information was the same for both types of students, teachers evaluated the attractive students more favorably than their unattractive peers. In addition, experimental studies indicate that such expectations can be communicated nonverbally, creating many pedagogical implications.

In a similar study, teachers received a report containing pictures with names and ages of both male and female students fictitiously said to be

"People seldom notice old clothes if you wear a big smile."

Lee Mildon

"The question is not what you look at, but what you see."

Henry David Thoreau

Teachers must believe and expect that all students can learn.

"Life is a matter of expectations."

Horace

"High achievement always takes place in the framework of high expectations."

Jack Kinder

"One can succeed at almost anything for which he has enthusiasm."

Charles Schwab

Teachers have a repertoire of nonverbal behaviors that affect students, both positively and negatively.

involved in a school disturbance. Previously, adult raters had judged each picture as either attractive or unattractive. Each teacher was asked to read the report, evaluate the seriousness of the disturbance, and give an impression of the student involved. When the disturbance was mild, the physical attractiveness of the student did not affect the teacher's reaction. When the misconduct was severe, however, teachers discerned that the behavior of unattractive boys and girls was chronically antisocial. On the other hand, teachers did not usually give this judgment for serious misconduct reported for attractive students. They tended to view the attractive students as normal and blamed the misbehavior on their having a bad day.

Research has also shown that teachers exhibit different nonverbal behaviors toward male and female students as well as students from different ethnic backgrounds. Both Caucasian and African American teachers appear to vary their nonverbal responses depending on the race and gender of students involved in the interaction. These studies support the need to ensure that teachers are sensitive to their own nonverbal behaviors when interacting with either males or females, or students from various ethnic groups.

Nonverbal communication can be a powerful tool used by teachers of disabled students. A study was conducted to determine whether teachers exhibited different nonverbal behaviors when presenting a lesson to students with varying intellectual and/or physical characteristics. Before presenting the lesson, teachers were given hypothetical information regarding the academic performance level for each student. In addition, teachers were not forewarned of the possibility of teaching a disabled student. A concealed camera recorded the lesson, and experts rated their nonverbal interaction.

Teachers must be sensitive to their own nonverbal behaviors when interacting with students.

"What we see depends mainly on what we look for."

John Lubbock

"Wise teachers create an environment that encourages students to teach themselves."

Leonard Roy Frank

Research has shown that teachers exhibit different nonverbal behaviors toward students from different ethnic backgrounds.

Positive teacher expectations bring positive student achievement.

"You have to expect things of yourself before you can do them."

Michael Jordan

"A master can tell you what he expects of you. A teacher, though, awakens your own expectations."

Patricia Neal

"We usually get what we anticipate."

Claude M. Bristol

The findings indicated that teachers exhibited more positive nonverbal behaviors toward students who were classified as non-disabled than toward those who were identified as disabled. The findings also indicated that teachers exhibited more favorable nonverbal behaviors toward students identified as high achievers than toward those identified as low achievers.

Specific examples of appropriate nonverbal forms of communication for the physically disabled (such as visually impaired and hearing impaired) and the learning disabled, as well as students with moderate/severe/profound mental retardation, have been suggested by numerous authors and researchers.

Based on the accumulated research concerning teacher expectations, educators should provide equal opportunities for all students to participate in classroom activities, be sensitive to differential treatment of high and low achievers, not allow low achievers to be isolated in groups, and believe and expect that all students can learn.

The bottom line for teachers is, whether intentional or not, nonverbal behavior tells students what we expect of them. Positive expectations bring positive achievements. Negative expectations bring loss of self-confidence and failure.

NONVERBAL AREAS

Facial Expressions

Facial expressions are the primary source of information next to words in determining an individual's internal feelings.

The adage "a picture is worth a thousand words" describes the effectiveness of facial expressions in the communication process. Facial appearance—including wrinkles, muscle tone, skin coloration, and eye color—offers cues that reveal information about age, race, and status. A less permanent second set of facial cues—including length of hair, hairstyle, cleanliness, and facial hair—often relate to an individual's idea of beauty. A third group of facial markers includes momentary expressions that signal emotions. Muscle movements that cause changes in the forehead, eyebrows, eyelids, cheeks, nose, lips, and chin—such as raising the eyebrows, wrinkling the brow, rolling the eyes, or curling the lip—register these expressions.

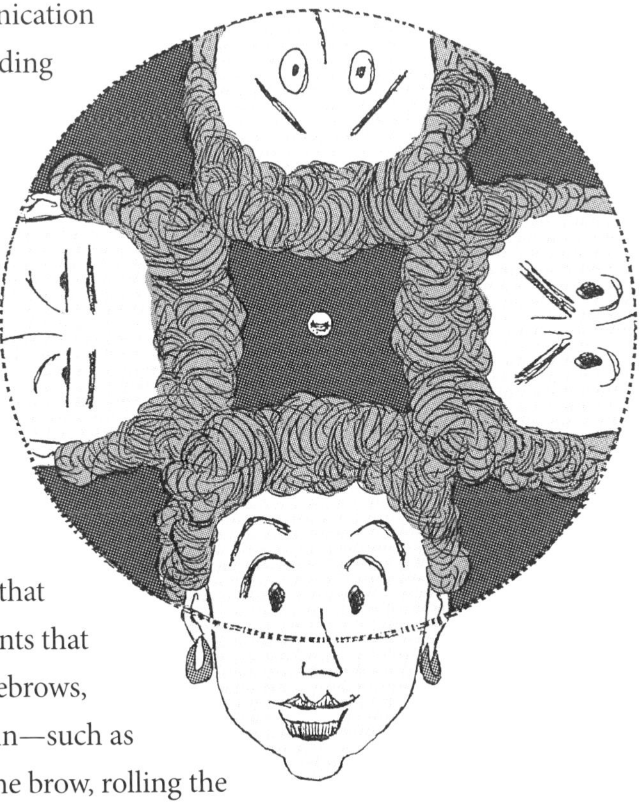

In human interaction, people focus their attention on the face to receive visual cues that support or contradict verbal messages. We send a great deal of information to others through involuntary and voluntary facial expressions.

"The face of a man gives us fuller and more interesting information than his tongue."

Arthur Schopenhauer

Fear causes involuntary facial expressions.

When truly frightened, people generally do not think about how to move facial muscles; therefore, the facial expression of fear is an example of an involuntary gesture.

Facial expressions can also be voluntary, such as when an individual wants to hide feelings. Such facial expressions are controlled for a number of reasons, but they are often dictated by societal or cultural standards or are a product of family rules. That "boys should never cry or look afraid" is a rule some members of our society ingrain in their children.

Attitudes toward others (e.g., interest or boredom, fear or anger, pleasure or displeasure) are vividly displayed through our emotions. People use this information to draw conclusions about our personality as well as other characteristics, which may or may not be true. For example, students with attractive faces are often judged by teachers to have more positive attributes than students with less attractive faces.

Attitudes toward other people and situations are vividly displayed through our emotions.

Some facial expressions are readily visible; others are so fleeting they go unnoticed. Both types can positively or negatively reinforce the spoken word and convey cues concerning emotions and attitude. Next to words, the human face is the primary source of information for determining an individual's internal feelings. However, researchers cannot reach a consensus on the universal meaning of any facial expression.

Facial expressions can be voluntary, such as when we want to deliberately hide our feelings.

Some physiologists contend that the face is capable of producing some 20,000 different expressions. Research has indicated that we display about 33 kinemes (individual movements) in our facial area.

Although research indicates that people of all cultures display similar facial cues for some emotions—such as happiness, fear, and surprise—culturally learned rules often trigger different responses. In most areas of the United States, a snake might stimulate reactions of fear or disgust.

"A man finds room in the few square inches of his face for all the traits of all his ancestors; for the expression of all his history, and his wants."

Ralph Waldo Emerson

"A smile is a curve that sets everything straight."

Phyllis Diller

People from all over the world exhibit comparable facial cues for many emotions. Cultural rules often trigger different facial responses.

In other places, however, the same reptile might elicit joy or excitement, as it might represent a culinary delicacy.

Smiles are the most widely understood positive facial expression, used all over the world to express happiness and pleasure. Smiles are rarely used deliberately, but may be used to mask other feelings. Consider a star athlete who loses to an opponent, but smiles to hide disappointment. Specific professionals that interact with the general public, such as flight attendants, are trained to use smiles to make tense moments more comfortable.

Facial expressions are sometimes used to meet social standards and hide true emotions. Consider the Miss USA pageant: the winner is the only contestant for whom it is okay to cry. Ironically, the losers are expected to be gracious, hiding disappointment and showing happiness for the winner. We all learn from experience—and with varying degrees of sophistication—to disguise our true feelings to fit socially acceptable standards.

In times of shock and mourning, we abandon pretenses. Our gestures and facial expressions accurately reflect emotions.

We often try to hide our feelings behind masks, which cannot conceal true emotions. Frowns, jutting chins, raised eyebrows, open mouths, and sneers can betray and ultimately broadcast deception. We are all capable of "faking" nonverbal communication—making happy or sad faces, smiles or frowns, but timing inevitably gives us away. We cannot determine how long to keep it on or how quickly to let it go. Thus, when trying to deliberately deceive others, we speak at slower rates, make more speech errors, and exhibit fewer head nods and more smiles.

Most people cannot hide true feelings and emotions behind facial masks.

A teacher's face should convey a variety of expressions when speaking to students. While listening to students, teachers should use facial expressions and eyes to communicate interest about questions and concerns. Remember that your primary role is to understand all of your students' needs so that you can provide appropriate instruction.

Whenever suitable, teachers should smile when working with students. Smiles present a warm and open invitation for communication. For some teachers, smiling comes naturally. Other teachers must make a conscious effort to put on a smile in front of students.

"If you smile when no one else is around, you really mean it."

Andy Rooney

Men and women display similar facial expressions.

It takes 17 facial muscles to smile and 43 to frown.

"Every time you smile at someone, it is an action of love, a gift to that person, a beautiful thing."

Mother Teresa

"I think your whole life shows in your face and you should be proud of that."

Lauren Bacall

Anger

Happiness

Fear

Eye Behavior

As the most dominant and reliable features of the face, eyes provide a constant channel of communication. They can be shifty and evasive, convey hate, fear, and guilt, or express confidence, love, and support. Studies show that eye behavior can be used to seek and provide information, regulate interaction, show attention and interest, influence others, and reveal attitudes.

Referred to as the mirrors of the soul, eyes serve as the major decision factor in deciphering the spoken truth. Statements used to express the awareness of eye behavior include "seeing is believing," "you are a sight for sore eyes," "I see what you mean," and "the eyes are the gateway to the mind." Eyes can be steely, knowing, mocking, piercing, or glowing. Eyes show moods and relationships (e.g., "a lover's gaze" or "a jealous competitor's stare.") Liars tend to avoid direct eye contact (e.g., "He couldn't look me in the eye" or "He had shifty eyes.")

Unlike other parts of the face, eyes can both send and receive messages. Except for extremely shy individuals, most people look for social acceptance by studying the eyes of others. Making eye contact communicates openness and honesty. Even a single glance will speak volumes.

Eyes also accurately indicate positive or negative relationships. People tend to look longer and more often at those whom they trust, respect, and care

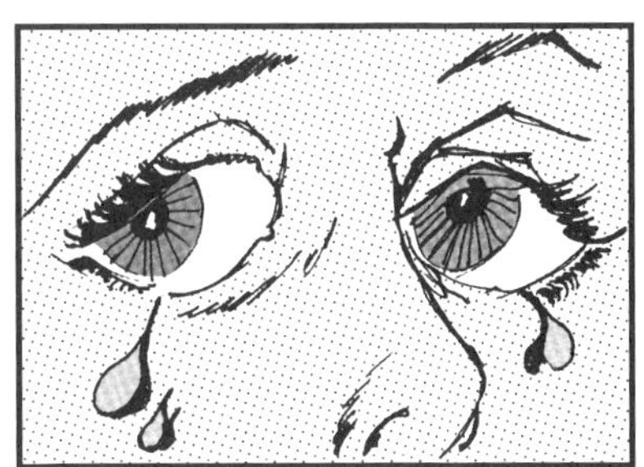

Eyes provide a constant channel of communication.

"With just a look or gesture... she would reveal to all of us... her compassion and her humanity."

Tony Blair during his eulogy for Princess Diana

"There is a sacredness in tears. They are not the mark of weakness, but of power. They speak more eloquently than ten thousand tongues. They are the messengers of overwhelming grief... and unspeakable love."

Washington Irving

Eye contact typically doesn't last longer than a few seconds before one or both people experience a strong inclination to look away.

"An eye can threaten like a loaded and levelled gun, or can insult like hissing or kicking; or, in its altered mood, by beams of kindness, it can make the heart dance with joy."

Ralph Waldo Emerson

"The eyes are not responsible when the mind does the seeing."

Publilius Syrus

about than at those whom they doubt or dislike. Thus, your eye contact will be more evident around people with whom you feel comfortable than with those whom you feel uneasy. It is ironic, however, that it's those we trust the least that we keep the closest eye on, or micromanage.

When someone avoids looking at you, it is often an indication that something is wrong. People avoid eye contact when they dislike or are not interested in someone. People with low self-esteem and people not telling the truth may also avoid making eye contact. Consider the context and cultural aspects before drawing any conclusion about lack of eye contact. For example, not looking someone in the eye does not always mean that someone is lying. We avert our eyes and do not make eye contact for a number of reasons (e.g., cultural, sadness, or shame) which may have nothing to do with lying. For example, it is a Japanese custom for a person of lesser title or standing to bow lower than a person of higher standing when introduced as a show of respect to avert ones eyes by bowing more deeply.

Normal eye dilation is not under the control of the individual. When looking at something pleasing, pupils will measurably dilate; when viewing something displeasing, pupils will constrict. Personality characteristics such as introversion/extroversion may also influence eye behavior. Professional poker players are cognizant of eye behavior and will often wear sunglasses to

When looking at something pleasing, pupils will measurably dilate.

prevent opponents from seeing their pupils dilate/constrict with a good/bad hand.

People in the United States typically associate eye contact with honesty, but in Japan people avoid eye contact as a sign of respect.

Eye contact can be manipulated to open or close channels of nonverbal communication. Most bell ringing fundraisers, for example, realize that lengthening eye contact increases their chances of getting a donation. A restaurant patron needing service knows that "catching" the server's eye is essential to obtaining fast service.

Eyes can be used as a good indicator of interest, or lack thereof, in a conversational topic. Eye behavior can control conversational roles—who should speak and who should listen. Thus, visual cues act as monitoring devices that regulate, coordinate, and control succession of speech. We indicate that we are paying attention to speakers by making eye contact with them. Maintaining appropriate eye contact encourages the speaker to continue to talk.

"The eyes of men converse as much as their tongues, with the advantage that the ocular dialect needs no dictionary, but is understood the entire world over. When the eyes say one thing, and the tongue another, a practiced man relies on the language of the first."

Ralph Waldo Emerson

"Catching" the server's eye is essential to obtaining fast service in a busy restaurant.

Teachers usually maintain eye contact and flash visual signals when they want to emphasize particular points. Students will often make eye contact with a teacher to indicate that they are paying attention to what the teacher has to say. Students who avoid eye contact may be indicating a lack of interest in the topic or teacher. Teachers should be cognizant of students' eyes and adjust or correct their method of instruction to gain the attention of all students.

Making eye contact exhibits a level of credibility and honesty.

Most experienced teachers are aware when students are bored with the subject matter being presented. Students' eyes often signal listening and non-listening behaviors. Students who are constantly looking at the wall clock rather than watching and listening to the teacher may be

---

"People only see what they are prepared to see."

Ralph Waldo Emerson

indicating the need for a break, the dullness of the content, or a lack of motivation and preparation. In any case, observation of student eye behavior can be used in evaluating teacher performance.

Sincerity is communicated more through eye behavior than through words.

Lack of student-teacher eye contact will often indicate disinterest, inattention, or even dislike for the teacher. Teachers should be aware of students who are looking down at the floor, staring out the window, or looking up at the ceiling and be quick to change the topic, ask questions, or take a break.

Direct teacher eye contact can also express support, disapproval, or neutrality. Numerous evaluation specialists suggest that a stern look should be the first form of action taken by a teacher to handle obvious cheaters in a testing situation. This direct eye contact usually serves as a powerful corrective measure in negating the wandering eyes of potential cheating students.

Experienced teachers look at students' eyes to gain their attention and to see how well they understand the subject matter being taught.

Teachers can have an individual connection with every student in the classroom by using eye contact.

Direct teacher eye contact can stop the wandering eyes of cheating students during a test.

Attitudes of intimacy, aloofness, concern, or indifference can be inferred by the way a teacher looks at or avoids looking at a student. Students also quickly learn to understand specific eye behavior—such as requesting an explanation or signifying the ending of a class period—communicated by the teacher. Students know from experience to avoid eye contact when the teacher poses a difficult question. The general rule is to stare downward or shuffle through notes, as if searching for the answer, to avoid opening channels of communication.

Students often avoid eye contact when asked a difficult question.

Teachers "teach to" students with friendly faces and attentive eyes. In turn, students convey interest in the subject matter by smiling and nodding their heads in agreement to the teacher's lesson.

Vocal Intonation

The adage "It is not what you say that counts, but how you say it" reflects the meaning of vocal intonation. Sometimes referred to as "paralinguistics," vocal intonation is probably the most easily understood area of nonverbal communication. It includes a multitude of components—such as rhythm, pitch, intensity, nasality, and slurring—that elicit the "truth" of a message. Vocal variations are fundamental components of expressive oral communication. If vocal intonation contradicts your words, the former will dominate.

Vocal intonation indicates the "truth" of a message.

"They may forget what you said, but they will never forget how you made them feel."

Carl W. Buechner

Vocal intonation—projection, variety, timing and rate of speech—influences how others perceive us and provides evidence about our self-confidence and enthusiasm. Vocal projection is the most important requisite to effective communication. If people cannot hear what you are saying, they will not be able to understand your message. Project your voice so students in the last row of seats

Vocal intonation can encourage or prevent students from responding to questions.

Your voice conveys meaning beyond words.

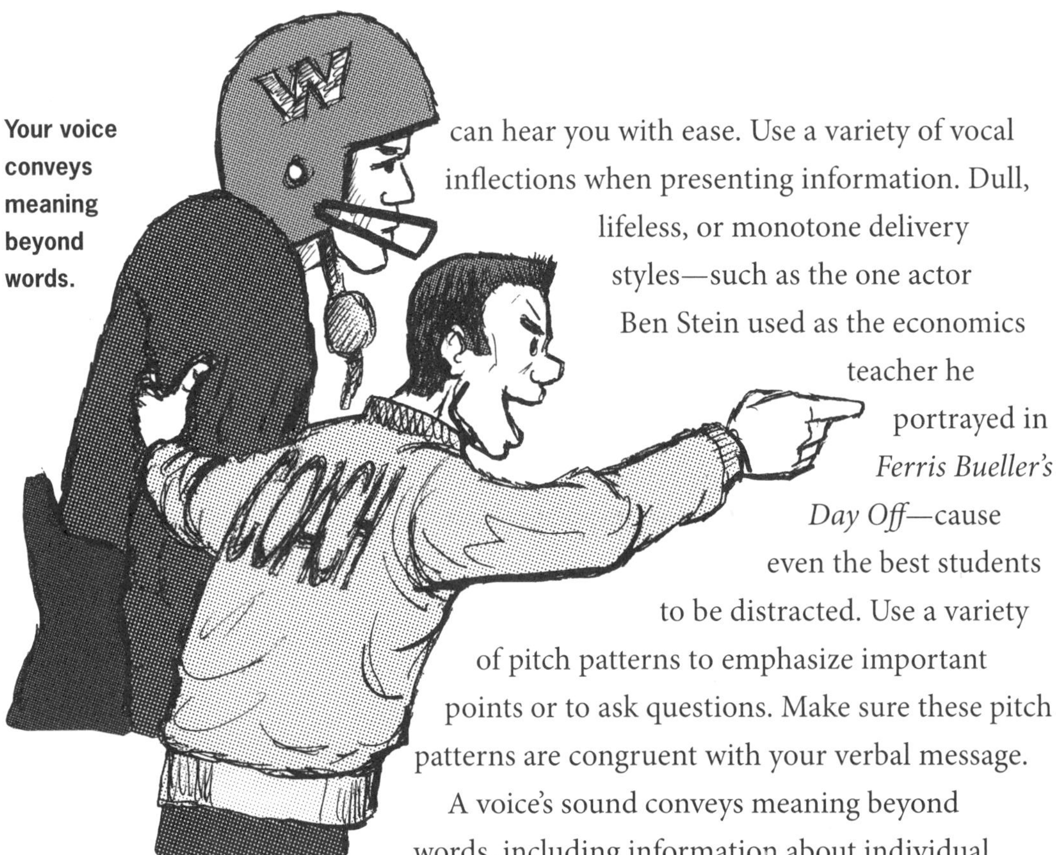

can hear you with ease. Use a variety of vocal inflections when presenting information. Dull, lifeless, or monotone delivery styles—such as the one actor Ben Stein used as the economics teacher he portrayed in *Ferris Bueller's Day Off*—cause even the best students to be distracted. Use a variety of pitch patterns to emphasize important points or to ask questions. Make sure these pitch patterns are congruent with your verbal message.

A voice's sound conveys meaning beyond words, including information about individual attributes such as age, emotional state or other personality characteristics. Tone, pitch, and speed affect the meaning of how words are sent and received. Vocal qualities are often influential where negative prejudice against certain paralinguistic styles is evident—for example, being annoyed when hearing a whining child. On the other hand, an unconscious bias of the listening public is a widespread positive prejudice in favor of men with low, deep voices with resonant tones, such as those qualities possessed by most male newscasters. Studies have also reported the use of vocal cues as accurate indicators of overall appearance, body type, height, education, and dialect region.

Your voice is an important barometer of how you feel about yourself, others, and the world around you.

"Language is wine upon the lips."

Virginia Woolf

CHILD

NEWSCASTER

Consider the resonant voice of Tom Brokaw, the deep and breathy voice of Sharon Stone, the nasal voice of Fran Drescher, and the thickly accented voice of Arnold Schwarzenegger.

We make judgments about age, gender, ethnicity, attractiveness, social class, and educational background based on voice qualities. We also make decisions about whether we believe or trust—and like or dislike—someone based on vocal characteristics.

Most people dislike the vocal qualities of a whining child, but favor the deep voices used by male newscasters.

"Everything becomes a little different as soon as it is spoken out loud."

Hermann Hesse

Anger is exemplified vocally by high pitch, fast pace, and blaring sound.

"Speak when you are angry, and you will make the best speech you will ever regret."

Laurence J. Peter

Paralinguistic cues also reveal emotional conditions. Differences in loudness, pitch, timbre, rate, inflection, rhythm, and enunciation all relate to the expression of various emotions. Research findings suggest that strong emotions, such as rage, are exemplified vocally by high pitch, fast pace, and blaring sound. Low pitch, retarded pace, and resonant sound portray more passive feelings, such as despair. In addition, stress is often vocalized by higher pitch with words uttered at a greater rate than normal. The reverse (lower pitch, slower word pace) is typical during depression. (See Table 1).

TABLE 1
CHARACTERISTICS OF VOCAL EXPRESSION

Vocal Attributes	Loudness	Pitch	Timbre	Rate	Inflection	Rhythm	Enunciation
Affection	Soft	Low	Resonant	Slow	Steady and slightly upward	Regular	Slurred
Anger	Loud	High	Blaring	Fast	Irregular up and down	Irregular	Clipped
Boredom	Moderate to low	Moderate to low	Moderately resonant	Moderately slow	Monotone or gradually falling	...	Somewhat slurred
Cheerfulness	Moderately high	Moderately high	Moderately blaring	Moderately fast	Up and down; over-all upward	Regular	...
Impatience	Normal	Normal to moderately high	Moderately blaring	Moderately fast	Slightly upward	...	Somewhat clipped
Joy	Loud	High	Moderately blaring	Fast	Upward	Regular	...
Sadness	Soft	Low	Resonant	Slow	Downward pauses	Irregular	Slurred
Satisfaction	Normal	Normal	Somewhat resonant	Normal	Slightly upward	Regular	Somewhat slurred

Davitz, J.R., (1976). ***The Communication of Emotional Meaning.***

The Nixon transcripts were difficult to judge because of the absence of vocal information.

VOCAL INTONATION

"Remember what you say comes back to you."

Zig Ziglar

"One of the lessons of history is that nothing is often a good thing to do and always a clever thing to say."

Will Durant

Richard Nixon demonstrated the importance of nonverbal communication when he sent transcripts rather than audiotapes of presidential conversations to the House Judiciary Committee in 1974. Committee members, considering possible impeachment and trying to determine the truth, complained that the "meaning" was not truly communicated because of the absence of voice modifications. Vocal information—intonation, tone, stress, length, and frequency of pauses—is lost when speech is transcribed.

Our voices can be used to say the same message in many different ways, ranging from bland disinterest to passionate intensity. The same words or phrases can have many different meanings, depending on how they are said. For example, analyze the phrase "thank you." If uttered sincerely, it generally means an expression of gratitude; if intoned sarcastically, it can insinuate an entirely opposite intention.

The same words or phrases can have many different meanings depending on how they are said.

Or if a mother asks a child to apologize for a wrongdoing, she often stresses that the child must "mean it." The mother expects more than the mere words "I'm sorry," and listens closely for vocal intonation to support the sincerity of the message.

Vocal intonation indicates the sincerity of a message.

Teachers should articulate words at a comfortable rate or pace in order to maximize the potential for student comprehension. Slow speaking teachers have a tendency to aggravate students, while fast/quick speaking teachers make it difficult for students to follow the lecture. Teachers should strive for a comfortable speaking pace that will vary in rhythm, inflection, and timbre in order to maintain students' interest. Experienced teachers know to use pauses to emphasize important points

A teacher's vocal intonation and other forms of body language modify students' behavior.

and provide adequate time for students to respond to questions. It is extremely important that teachers strive for clear, correct diction, and articulation of every word so all students understand instructional content.

"How well we communicate is determined not by how well we say things but by how well we are understood."

Andrew Grove

Consider a situation in which the teacher asks a question and calls on a talented student, who answers the question correctly. Generally, the teacher responds with positive verbal reinforcement enhanced by vocal pitch or tone, expressing acceptance of the student's answer (often accompanied by a smile or other forms of nonverbal approval). In the same situation, if the teacher called on a less talented student whose response was incorrect, not only might the teacher verbally reject the response, but also the teacher might hinder future responses from this student because of the accompanying negative vocal cues.

When delivering a message, teachers should change their rate of speech throughout the conversation for emphasis, using inflection and moderate changes in pitch and volume to maintain student attention. When teachers mumble, stutter, or bellow, their messages are less effective.

Teachers should be cognizant of the rate, articulation, projection, and inflection of verbal messages sent to students. Teachers can follow several guidelines to improve their vocal messages, such as:

- varying vocal pitch and inflection to emphasize important points of a lesson,
- conveying interest and energy through the voice when teaching,
- speaking loud enough so all students can hear what is communicated,
- pacing delivery so all students have an opportunity to conceptualize material,
- using the voice to present a sense of confidence and assurance,
- using simple sentences to present instructional material, and
- using appropriate tone when asking questions.

Teachers should be aware of the rate, articulation, projection, and inflection of verbal messages sent to students.

"We cannot learn from one another until we stop shouting at one another—until we speak quietly enough so that our words can be heard as well as our voices."

Richard M. Nixon

"The true genius shudders at incompleteness—and usually prefers silence to saying something which is not everything it should be."

Edgar Allan Poe

Touching is appropriate when congratulating students for some achievement or success.

Touching

Touching is an important aspect of any culture. Even a handshake can tell much about an individual's character. Our skin has hundreds of thousands of submicroscopic nerve endings that serve as tactual receptors, detecting pressure, temperature, and texture.

During a job interview, an applicant whose handshake barely clasps the finger tips of the potential employer may indicate that the person is too timid for a sales position. On the other hand, a "death grip" handshake, in which the applicant squeezes the potential employer's hand, may indicate the person is overbearing and insensitive. Physical touch and warmth are remembered through the handshaking tradition. We vividly recall impressions made by individuals who had a warm and powerful handshake as well as those who had a cold and "dead fish" handshake. Our memory of these tactual contacts leaves as much of a lasting impression as the words spoken and other nonverbal messages.

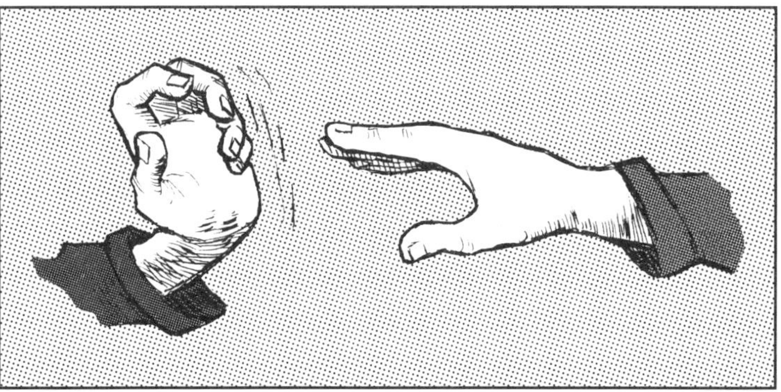

Our skin has thousands of tactual receptors.

"You cannot shake hands with a clenched fist."

Indira Gandhi

Considered by many to be the most primitive form of communication, tactual sensitivity begins in childhood with a baby's first cuddling from its mother, and it greatly contributes to the mental and emotional adjustment of the individual. In fact, traditional methods of birth are a shock because of the "coldness" of moving the infant from a warm, secure womb to a sanitary bassinet. This sudden assault after removal from the mother's body may be a serious mistake. Methods, such as Lamaze, provide gentler transitions to foster natural birth and emphasize the importance of touching. Babies themselves find comfort in the feel of their blankets and excitement in items warm and cold, smooth and rough.

Parents communicate to an infant physically through touching.

Parents transmit their feelings to an infant physically, not verbally. Parents may say "I love you," but the words do not communicate. Babies are unable to talk and to understand words spoken to them, but they can communicate most effectively and meaningfully what they feel. The period between 11 and 18 months is a critical time for infants. During this early stage of development, babies go through a transition from pre-linguistic to linguistic communication. The behavioral development of babies deprived of loving

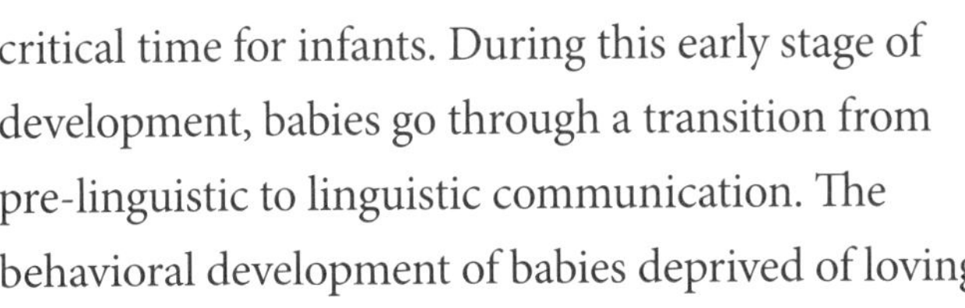

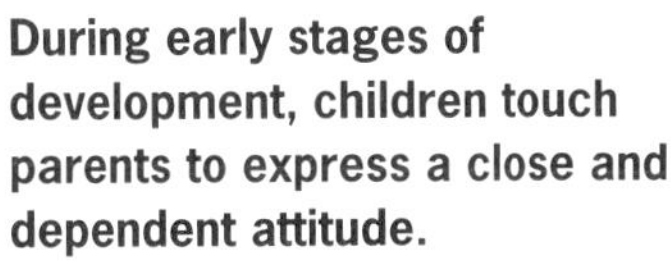

During early stages of development, children touch parents to express a close and dependent attitude.

TOUCHING BY...

CHILDREN

ADOLESCENTS

Tactual experiences are used as primary awareness tools to discover and learn until societal inhibitions are imposed to curtail or alter these behaviors.

and tactual experiences can be stunted and result in a variety of health problems (such as allergies and eczema).

As infants grow older, they still use tactual experiences as primary awareness tools to discover and learn until societal inhibitions are imposed to curtail or alter these behaviors.

Until 10 to 12 years of age, children touch parents to express close and dependent attitudes, whereas they touch peers generally to express affiliation or aggression. At adolescence, touching is reduced to the extent that little of it occurs between parent and child beyond the hands and arms.

In general, the meaning of touching depends on the situation, culture, gender, and age.

In general, the meaning of touching depends on the situation, culture, gender, and age. In most cases, casual touching between adults in the United States is less common than in other cultures. Because tactual experiences are considered private, we often go out of our way to avoid making physical contact with strangers.

Our non-touching society directly relates to the concept of self; people feel that their bodies and clothing are "off limits" except under certain socially accepted conditions. These include sexual encounters with spouses or partners; touching between parents and children up to adolescence;

greetings and farewells with friends and relatives (handshakes and hugs); providing sympathy for people in mental or physical pain; "examination-related" touching by doctors and other healthcare professionals; and contact in specifically designed encounter groups where the primary purpose is therapy.

In most relationships, touching can give encouragement, express tenderness, and show emotional support. The right to touch is largely determined by status. People who are older, richer, or hold a superior position may acceptably touch those who are younger, poorer, or in a subordinate position. For this reason, status could prohibit a teacher from touching an administrator.

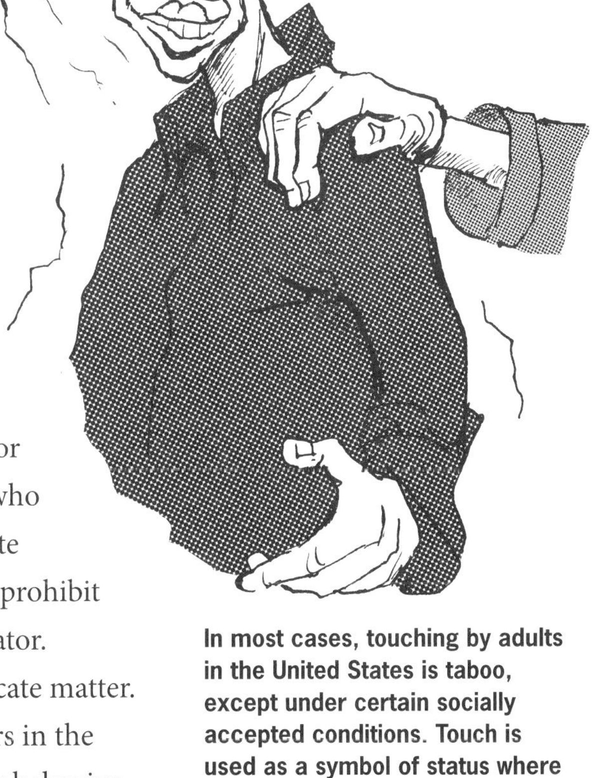

In most cases, touching by adults in the United States is taboo, except under certain socially accepted conditions. Touch is used as a symbol of status where superiors may touch inferiors, but the reverse is not likely.

Touching in the classroom is a delicate matter. Since teachers are considered superiors in the classroom, they often initiate touching behavior. Although perhaps warranted, a teacher who grabs the arm or shoulder of a student who is misbehaving in the classroom enters the student's space uninvited, creating an uncomfortable and awkward situation.

More positively, touching can also be used to reinforce. Teachers can develop closer relationships

Patting a student on the arm, shoulder, or back is a common form of encouragement and support.

"Too often we underestimate the power of a touch, a smile, a kind word, a listening ear, an honest compliment, or the smallest act of caring, all of which have the potential to turn a life around."

Leo F. Buscaglia

with their students by entering into their space. Simple pats on the back for jobs well done are a much used—and usually favorably accepted—form of praise. Research has indicated that small children tend to learn significantly more when teachers exhibit touching, close body proximity, and smiles of approval. As children grow older, however, touching behaviors become less appropriate.

Body Movements and Gestures

Kinesics refers to body movements, and these movements communicate meaning. Our bodies elucidate true messages about feelings that cannot be masked. Body movements and gestures can enhance your credibility or can rob you of your confidence. We communicate by the way we walk, stand, sit, what we do with our shoulders, hands, arms, and legs, how we hold our heads, and the manner in which we position our bodies toward or away from others.

When happy, we tend to walk vigorously; conversely, when sad, we often slouch and drag our feet when walking.

Posture often indicates mood and attitude. When happy, we tend to walk vigorously (e.g., John Travolta's character Tony Manero's "strut" as he walks down a Brooklyn street carrying a bucket of paint in the beginning of *Saturday Night Fever);* conversely, when "down in the dumps," we often slouch, bow our heads with eyes focused down, and walk with a sluggish pace. An individual's stride and pace will indicate a variety of meanings from confidence to ineptitude. Generally, people who walk rapidly present a message of being goal-oriented, while people who scuff along with heads down signal sadness.

We communicate by the way we walk, stand, and sit.

"Your body doesn't know how to lie."

Julius Fast

An individual's stride and pace will indicate a variety of meanings from confidence to ineptitude.

The body tends to move in harmony with words. As people converse with each other, they are often in unison—frequently with similar postural configurations.

The power of body movements is exemplified in foreign movies when English words are dubbed in with subtitles. No matter how well the words are synchronized with lip movements, the actors' body movements and gestures are often awkward.

Crime prevention experts reveal that muggers look for victims that walk with a disinterested posture—with shoulders and heads down, unaware of their surroundings. A mugger does not want to attack someone who appears alert and prepared.

UNAWARE

Crime experts suggest that muggers are looking for victims whose body movements and posture suggest unawareness of surroundings.

We express attitudes toward others vividly through our body movements and gestures. Experimental findings indicate that postural relaxation of torso and limbs can denote status or strength in a relationship. People tend to be more relaxed with friends or when addressing those of lower status. On the other hand, they will be less relaxed with strangers or when addressing those of superior status.

ALERT

Body orientation (the degree to which a listener's legs and shoulders face in the direction of the speaker) indicates status or liking of an individual. If your body orientation is more toward a person, chances are you have a positive attitude about him or her. When bored or disinterested, you may be inclined to turn your head or entire body away from the speaker.

People tend to be more relaxed with friends or when interacting with individuals of lower status.

Although the human body is fashioned similarly throughout the world, postural differences vary tremendously from culture to culture. While there are more than one thousand body orientations to choose from, the postural choices you choose to make are usually determined by cultural influences.

We lean forward when we like someone. On the other hand, we lean away from individuals we have negative attitudes toward.

Twenty-five percent of the world's population prefers to squat rather than sit in chairs.

People in the United States have such a narrow postural vocabulary that they often have a difficult time accepting postural ranges found in other countries. For example, 25 percent of the world's population prefers to squat, whereas this is an awkward position for most adults in the United States who typically prefer to sit in chairs.

Body movements are frequently indicators of self-confidence, energy, fatigue and/or status. Body movements can also indicate a person's mood or emotional state. A happy person will often carry a more erect posture than will someone who is depressed, shy, or submissive. Body posture can be accurately observed at a distance. For example, we can often identify someone we know from a distance simply by the walking posture they use.

Body posture can indicate a person's position or status within a group.

Posture sometimes will give away a person's position or status within a group. People of equal status will often show similarity in postures they adopt. For example, if one person of equal status in the group is sitting in a chair leaning back, chances are good that others of equal status will mimic that

People with good rapport will often adopt similar body posture.

posture. Friends or people in agreement will also generally mirror each other's posture. This tendency to echo postures is especially evident where there is a high degree of rapport. On the other hand, people can deliberately adopt postures different than others within the group to show difference or dissension. Lower status individuals within a group are often shown bowing their heads and holding their body in a less than erect position. Higher status individuals will often use a more erect posture to indicate their dominance within a group.

In the classroom, students receive nonverbal messages of enthusiasm or boredom communicated through a teacher's body orientation. Students sense confidence or frustration from these unconscious behaviors of the teacher.

Students send messages to teachers about their interest in the class through body postures and movements.

An observant teacher can also tell when students understand material presented or when students have trouble grasping major concepts. Slouching in a chair sends a very different nonverbal message than leaning forward or sitting erect. Slumping often indicates fatigue, boredom, discouragement, and tiredness. When seated, attentive students will sit up straight and lean slightly toward the teacher to indicate interest in the topic.

A student's posture will often indicate enthusiasm.

Orientating yourself away from the speaker will often convey detachment or disagreement, regardless of the words being spoken.

Body language provides subtle messages, which are subconsciously interpreted by others.

"See how she leans her cheek upon her hand! O that I were a glove upon that hand, that I might touch that cheek!"

Romeo in William Shakespeare's play *Romeo and Juliet*

Gestures—usually made with hands—are used in a variety of situations. Teachers routinely use gestures to convey information to students. Gestures are typically made unconsciously to support or contradict verbal messages.

Gestures are often comprehended more quickly than speech. They are preferred when communication is essential, such as during moments of stress. As a visual form of communication, gestures travel much farther than spoken words and are unaffected by the presence of noise that can sometimes interrupt or cancel out speech. Gestures can either add to or replace words.

Examples of common gestures include:

- raising a hand to gain attention,
- clapping to show approval or excitement,
- yawning to show boredom,
- nodding the head to show agreement with what is being said,
- patting someone on the back for encouragement,
- shrugging shoulders to convey "I don't know," "I don't care," or "I am not sure,"
- steepling (the finger tips are placed together in what resembles an attitude of prayer except the palms are kept apart) to signify confidence,
- resting hands on hips to assert control, and
- folding arms across the chest to indicate defensiveness, withdrawal, or self-protection.

Always analyze body gestures within a specific context to decipher the real meaning of the message. A gesture may have a specific meaning in one context and no meaning in another. For example, folded arms may be done in an effort to stay warm due to the cold temperature in a room and have nothing to do with being defensive or withdrawn. Other clues—such as tightness of the rest of the body—must be examined in order to validate the general interpretation of resistance. Also keep in mind that a gesture may have specific meaning in one culture and a completely different meaning in another culture.

It is very important that teachers learn how to use natural body movements when talking in front of a class of students. Inappropriate postures and gestures will diminish a lesson's delivery. All body movements should be used to accentuate and confirm verbal messages. The best way for teachers to check body movements, postures, and gestures is to record themselves teaching an actual class. Ask colleagues or friends to view the recording and point out weaknesses that you can attempt to eliminate in the future.

Body movements, postures, and gestures alone have no exact meaning, but they can greatly support or reject the spoken word. If these two means of communication contradict each other, the result will be a distorted image and most often the nonverbal will dominate.

We judge others more by what they do than by what they say.

"There's language in her eye, her cheek, her lip. Nay her foot speaks; her wanton spirits leak out at every joint and motive of her body."

Ulysses in William Shakespeare's play *Troilus and Cressida*

"It's a mistake to think we listen only with our ears. It's much more important to listen with the mind, the eyes, the body, and the heart."

Mark Herndon

Personal space plays an important part in nonverbal communication. Enough space can make us feel relaxed whereas too little can make us feel anxious.

Use of space

The use of space, or proxemics, is a subtle component of body language that indicates territory to which access is allowed or denied to other people or objects. Hall (1969) identified three types of space:

- *Fixed-feature space* (immovable walls or partitions and objects),
- *Semi-fixed-feature space* (big objects, such as chairs and tables), and
- *Informal space* (personal space around individuals).

Fixed-feature space. The layout of walls or partitions and other immovable objects affects learning that takes place in classrooms. The findings and implications of a controlled experiment conducted more than forty years ago remain relevant in many of today's classrooms. The study dealt with the effect of different aesthetic room qualities on students' ratings of photographs of faces based on dimensions of "energy" and "well-being." Students were placed in one of three rooms—a beautiful room, an ugly room, and an average room. The beautiful room had two large windows with drapes, beige walls, indirect overhead lighting, and

The use of space indicates territory to which access is allowed or denied to other people or objects.

Fixed-feature space involves the layout of partitions and immovable objects that affect the learning environment.

attractive furnishings; the ugly room had two half-windows, battleship gray walls, an overhead bulb with a soiled lampshade, and furnishings to give the impression of a dirty storeroom; the average room (an office) had three windows with shades, gray walls, indirect overhead lighting, and reasonably attractive furnishings. Subjects in the beautiful room rated the faces significantly higher than those in either of the other two rooms. Responses in the average room more closely resembled those in the ugly room than those in the beautiful room.

A follow-up study to determine if the results were long-lasting increased participants' time in both the beautiful and the ugly rooms from the original ten minutes to eight hours (four 1-hour sessions and two 2-hour sessions). The findings were dramatic: participants in the ugly room had reactions of monotony, fatigue, headaches, irritability, and hostility; those in the beautiful

Classroom layout and aesthetics can directly impact students' learning.

Fixed-feature space includes walls and other immovable objects.

ENVIRONMENT AFFECTS STUDENTS' ATTITUDES

room responded favorably with feelings of comfort, pleasure, importance, and enjoyment for completing the assigned tasks.

The implications concerning fixed-feature spatial environments for today's classrooms are obviously important, considering that students spend about six hours a day, five days a week, and forty weeks a year in these learning environments. Clearly, the physical classroom environment can create moods and influence how much communication takes place.

Classroom environments can create moods and establish how much communication takes place.

"Every part of the school environment affects character, for good or for ill."

Thomas Lickona

Semi-fixed feature space. Physical arrangement of furniture (especially chairs, desks, and tables) also dictates special boundaries and effectively communicates through subtle channels. Most schools lack imagination and creativity regarding elements that could easily be manipulated to make classroom environments more enjoyable. Despite recent teaching innovations, many classroom settings remain the same, with dark and dismal interiors.

The position of a teacher's desk may serve as a barrier to prevent students from entering her/his space and thus inhibits interaction.

Space in the classroom may also serve to indicate status, dominance, and leadership. The higher the professional status of the person, the more space he/she is awarded. The position of a teacher's desk may act as a barricade to prevent students from entering her/his space and thus inhibits interaction. Classroom decor reflects style and level of professionalism. Personal items and decorating provide clues to personality and lifestyle.

Semi-fixed feature space involves the arrangement of furniture.

Students frequently use space to send a message about their interest in a topic by sitting in the front or the back of a classroom. Researchers have found that straight-row seating, which originally evolved to make optimum use of natural lighting from windows, greatly affects involvement in the process of communication. The location of students in typical straight-row seating is a major factor in determining which students the teacher talks with, and which students respond to the teacher. With such an arrangement, student interaction is greatest in the front and middle rows, whether seating is imposed or self-selected.

In straight-row seating, most student interaction is greatest in the front and middle rows.

Students spend about six hours a day, five days a week, and forty weeks a year in classroom environments.

Informal space. From childhood on, you learn the meanings of thousands of spatial cues. Most adults in the United States have been reared with the understanding that a precise amount of space must exist when two people communicate.

Personal space is the social distance in which we do not expect strangers to intrude. This personal space bubble is invisible to us and to others, but it is very real. The amount of space required to feel comfortable varies from culture to culture and individual to individual. This personal "space bubble" changes size and shape, depending on the situation.

Four categories of informal space have been established in the United States:

- *Intimate*—Reserved for close relationships, sharing, protecting, and comforting;
- *Personal*—Used for informal conversations between friends occur in this 1½ - to 4-foot zone;
- *Social*—Accepted for interaction between strangers, teachers and students, and business acquaintances; typically happens within a 4- to 12-foot distance; and
- *Public*—Used for such one-way communication as exhibited by lecturers and tends to be between 12 and 25 feet (Hall, 1969).

Adults in the United States have a personal space bubble that changes size and shape depending on the situation.

Each culture has rules that dictate how close or far one person must stand or sit from another. Whereas other cultures rely on proximity to decipher honesty, adults in the United States accept closeness only for intimate relationships. From early childhood, we are taught to avoid body contact with strangers. Many nonverbal cues such as eye contact, body gestures, and facial expressions limit the space between individuals.

Informal space is the distance between you and other people or objects.

No one is comfortable in a crowded subway car or elevator with strangers invading our space and touching our bodies. Normally, we look straight ahead and avoid making eye contact. As others invade our personal space, we will move away from them to maintain an acceptable social distance. If we invade the personal space of others, they will back away to maintain an acceptable distance. If you sit too close to someone on a public bench, you can actually cause him or her to move away from you until they feel more comfortable. Other cultures (e.g., Middle East, Latin America, and Southern Europe) have a much smaller social distance that would be considered impolite in the United States.

People tend to get closer to those they like and maintain a greater distance from those they dislike, fear, or those to whom they are inferior.

Most people tend to get closer to those they like and maintain a greater distance from those they dislike or fear. People also stand farther away from those with disabilities, those from different racial backgrounds, and authority figures.

The distance between a teacher and students is a critical factor in the communication process.

Teachers share feelings of acceptance or rejection by the distance they maintain between themselves and their students.

Teachers can easily share feelings of acceptance or rejection simply by the distance they maintain. They have "freedom of space" whereas students do not. Teachers, as well as others, have a tendency to get closer to those they like.

The most advanced curriculum and the highest hopes have little chance of success without a supportive physical learning environment. The teacher must allow for flexible changes that are beneficial for group interaction. It should be noted that appropriate spatial distances and arrangements are limited by a myriad of variables including conversational topic, the nature of the relationship, and the physical constraints present in the classroom.

Teachers have freedom to move around in the classroom whereas students do not.

Dress identifies gender, age, socioeconomic class, status, role, group membership, physical climate, and time in history.

Dress

Charles Darwin refuted the notion that humans wear clothing mainly for protection from the elements. Often dictated by societal norms, clothing indicates a great amount of information. It identifies gender, age, socioeconomic class, status, role, group membership, personality or mood, physical climate, occupation, and time in history. Although most people are only superficially aware of the attire of others, clothing does communicate. Colors and fabrics are coordinated to send messages just as words are put together to form sentences. Dress can either alienate or persuade. Appropriate dress is a method of expressing respect for both the particular situation and the people in it: hence the need for leisure clothes and work clothes. Overtly, as with the hippies of the 1960s and 1970s, attire can be used to demonstrate dissension or refusal to accept the status game.

Throughout history, clothing has served as a status symbol. Kings wore purple, clergy dressed in black, and today gangs use colors to represent their groups. Generally, higher status individuals are associated with more expensive, higher-quality

---

"I base most of my fashion taste on what doesn't itch."

Gilda Radner

"Good clothes open all doors."

Thomas Fuller

apparel. Some executives and politicians wear a red tie—the power tie—and expensive suits or dresses to promote a sense of power, confidence, and assertive behaviors when interacting with others.

Throughout history, clothing has served as a status symbol.

Traditionally, distinctive costumes were worn to indicate rigid hierarchical groups. Today's changing Western culture does not follow these "tagging patterns." Historical dress used to denote gender categories. Now, the working environment usually dictates dress and the business suit, once meant for the executive only, is appropriate dress for both men and women in the business world. Clothing may also be age-graded. Some garments such as the miniskirt and bikini are considered more acceptable for younger women and are therefore seldom worn by older women.

Appearance counts. You must look the part to be perceived as credible. Image is a silent factor often used in business to hire and promote. Your appearance shouts or whispers a vast amount of information about you. Your attire should fit the professional image.

You are never judged solely on what you do. Your clothes and the image you project nonverbally communicate and leave an impression.

"Fashion passes, style remains."

Coco Chanel

CLOTHING

Working environments usually dictate appropriate professional dress.

What you wear makes a statement about you and your position within an organization. It is often an unwritten policy that your dress, including accessories and hairstyle, match your position. A new employee must quickly learn the organization's dress codes and follow them to be thought of as a team player. As part of your effort to succeed in any new job, make a mental note of the dress of colleagues at your level. Pay attention to the details such as the type, color, and style of clothes, shoes, and accessories worn by co-workers. Once the dress code is understood, dress in a similar manner in order to be considered part of the team.

"Clothes make the man. Naked people have little or no influence on society."

Mark Twain

DRESS

Much research has been completed about the effect of clothing on others. Clothing can reflect the personality, attitudes, and values of the wearer. Some people use clothing for decoration and self-expression; others are concerned with economy or comfort. Self-expression and ideal self-image are often vividly expressed by the selection of apparel.

An interesting study examined female subjects' descriptions of the characteristics of popular women. Clothing was found to be second in importance to personality; physical appearance, which is obviously altered by clothing, was third. Clunky jewelry, garish makeup and overpowering cologne speak volumes without saying a word. Moderation and thoughtful usage are key.

Clothing reflects your attitudes, values, and personality.

"Clothes don't make the man, but clothes have got many a man a good job."

Herbert Harold Vreeland

"I'm interested in longevity, timelessness, style—not fashion."

Ralph Lauren

A teacher's attire can help to establish credibility. Reasonableness is the guide for appropriate teacher attire.

"Fashion is a form of ugliness so intolerable that we have to alter it every six months."

Oscar Wilde

"If men run the world, why can't they stop wearing neckties? How intelligent is it to start the day by tying a little noose around your neck?"

Linda Ellerbee

Because clothing affects others' perceptions, people often dress to fit the part. These clothing cues, however, have little influence on those with whom you are familiar. Thus, if you overtly alter a style of dress, those who know you usually think it is a mood change rather than a permanent change of personality or values.

Stipulations for teachers to dress professionally or appropriately are subjective and leave wide gaps for interpretation. Thirty years ago, most teachers wore a coat and tie or blouse and skirt, but today's teachers have a much more relaxed attitude.

Teachers should dress to fit organizational standards. In absence of clear dress codes, teachers should be aware of possible interpretations made by students, faculty, parents, and administrators. Research has shown that students will accept teachers who dress reasonably smart and conventional as experts in their subject areas more than teachers who dress casually.

Teachers often underestimate the influence they have on students in the classroom without even speaking. Students notice what teachers wear and have been known to judge teachers' competence by how well they dress professionally.

What is considered acceptable attire differs from place to place, making it difficult to translate appropriate dress policies across geographical borders. What is acceptable attire for teachers in suburban California will not necessarily be the same as what is expected in rural Kentucky or northern Maine. Appropriate attire for teachers in some school districts is negotiated as part of a union contract while in other school districts a school board may develop specific policies.

Appropriate attire guidelines for teachers usually cover jewelry, dresses, skirts, hosiery, shorts, pants, suits, and shoes. Attire may also take into consideration makeup, facial hair, body piercings (other than earrings), and tattoos. Teachers should understand appropriate attire without needing an itemized list of acceptable and unacceptable clothing styles. Attire guidelines may also consider inclement weather conditions and special class activities as circumstances when teachers may "dress down."

Think of attire in theatrical terms. The teacher (actor) must be costumed to fit the curriculum (play) and the classroom (setting). In order to establish credibility, you should strive to appear comfortable and at ease in the role, thus removing some of the typical teacher/student barriers.

Outward appearance does not, of course, indicate a teacher's knowledge, values, or philosophy. But dress can communicate. Students see teachers based on their motivation, sincerity, and fairness; clothing will fool them only momentarily. A Savile Row suit or a Givenchy dress cannot turn a grouch into a lively, dynamic teacher. A smile is worth much more than what the teacher might pay for clothes.

There is considerable evidence in the realm of public speaking that your appearance affects how your audience will respond to you and your message.

"Good teaching is one-fourth preparation and three-fourths theater."

Gail Godwin

"You get the best out of others when you give the best of yourself."

Harry Firestone

Students judge teachers based on their motivation, sincerity, and fairness; clothing will fool them only momentarily.

FINAL COMMENTS

If effective communication is to be achieved in today's schools, it must be an open process where teachers and students possess the ability to send and receive messages accurately. A good teacher is a good listener, not only to words being spoken, but also to silent messages that signal agreement/disagreement, attention/inattention, interest/boredom, and the desire of the student to be heard. Nonverbal effectiveness is generally characterized by showing enthusiasm, varying facial expressions, gesturing for emphasis, moving toward students, maintaining eye contact, displaying positive head nods, and speaking with a clear voice and varied intonation.

Teachers should use positive gestures to congratulate students.

"I touch the future. I teach."

Christa McAuliffe

Knowledge is transmitted through effective communication and nurtured by skillfully sending and receiving messages in a variety of situations. Nonverbal behaviors must be learned and practiced. These behaviors include fostering positive characteristics, mannerisms, actions, and

"Communication works for those who work at it."

John Powell

habits, as well as overcoming negative ones that depress an atmosphere for learning.

Viewing a recording of your teaching can provide you with nonverbal feedback that is beneficial to both the beginning and veteran teacher. Screen the recording for facial expressions and eye behavior when interacting with students, spatial distance maintained between students, and the use of body movements and gestures. Enlist the aid of others to provide feedback about the appropriateness of nonverbal actions in the classroom and suggestions to improve your nonverbal interactions with students in the future.

Galloway (1972) suggested ten dimensions for judging student nonverbal behaviors:

Congruity/Incongruity refers to the consistency and inconsistency of verbal and nonverbal elements communicated by a teacher. Congruity occurs when the nonverbal messages support and reinforce verbal messages; a mixed message or incongruity exists when there is a discrepancy or contradiction between these two channels.

Teachers should ensure that their verbal and nonverbal messages are congruent.

Teachers should be aware of students' eye behavior and other nonverbal feedback.

Responsive/Unresponsive refers to modifications in teacher behavior in response to student feedback. A responsive act occurs when a teacher's reactions or responses are appropriate to the nonverbal student feedback (e.g., altering the instructional delivery pattern because of student misunderstanding of lesson content). Unresponsive acts are identified by lack of teacher responsiveness to student feedback, either by ignoring or being insensitive to student actions.

Positive/Negative Affectivity refers to expressions exhibited by a teacher to reinforce student behaviors. Positive affective expressions

"The single biggest problem in communication is the illusion that it has taken place."

George Bernard Shaw

If our words say one thing and our body language says another, most people will believe how we act more than what we say.

A teacher's actions can reinforce or thwart student behavior or student interaction.

"It is my business to know things. Perhaps I have trained myself to see what others overlook."

Sherlock Holmes in Sir Arthur Conan Doyle's book *A Case of Identity*

include warm feelings, high regard, cheerful enthusiasm, and acceptance. Negative affective expressions include aloofness, coldness, low regard, indifference, and rejection.

Attentive/Inattentive refers to a teacher's ability to listen to student messages. Attentiveness implies listening with patience and interest; inattentiveness implies disinterest in or failure to encourage students' verbal or nonverbal behavior.

Facilitating/Unreceptive refers to a teacher's response to students' needs and/or problems. A facilitator encourages students to share problems and responds positively to them. An unreceptive teacher openly ignores or responds inappropriately to students' needs and/or problems.

Supportive/Disapproving refers to actions exhibited by a teacher to reinforce or thwart student behavior or student interaction. Supportive teacher behaviors include encouragement and praise. Disapproving behaviors express dissatisfaction and discouragement.

Intimate/Distant refers to contact between a teacher and students. Intimacy is characterized by the presence of a psychological and physical closeness; distance by the absence of physical contact, by withdrawal, or by "cold" treatment.

Inclusive/Exclusive refers to nonverbal behaviors exhibited by a teacher to include or exclude students. Inclusion is evident when mutual glances and acknowledgments foster communicative exchange. Exclusion is a lack of recognition or disregard for the student's presence.

Free Time/Restrictive Time refers to the use of time with others, including the quality of time spent with students.

Open Space/Closed Space refers to travel routes and territorial rights in the classroom. Student accessibility to space in a school or classroom fosters openness, whereas denying access to these areas restricts.

Teachers should be aware of their travel routes in the classroom.

Successful teachers incorporate positive nonverbal communication in their teaching methodology. Examples of nonverbal tips for teachers include:

Quickly learn the names of your students and proper pronunciations. Students will be more responsive in class if they believe you care about them as individuals. Because names are related to ethnic backgrounds, proper pronunciation and voice inflection are important. Knowing all students' names might also dispel the notion that grades are dispersed on the basis of who knows the teacher best.

Show your approval. There is nothing so motivating as a nod or smile. You'll find that students' work improves and progress quickens.

"The way we communicate with others and with ourselves ultimately determines the quality of our lives."

Anthony Robbins

There is nothing as motivating as a smile.

Use supplementary teaching materials with clear directions, correct spellings, and illustrative examples. Students interpret such material as an extension of you and your teaching. Don't tolerate your own mistakes, and you'll find fewer from your students.

Be enthusiastic no matter what the topic. Come to class prepared and focused. Students usually imitate their instructors and will follow your lead. Approach elementary projects explaining their simplicity but emphasizing the underlying lesson. Use your nonverbal skills to make lectures more interesting. Thinking again in theatrical terms, a teacher is much like an actor. When the curtain goes up the instructor must captivate the audience. Important aspects of both acting and teaching include not only the script but also meaningful use of gestures, expressions, vocal variations and intonations, eye contact, and multiple other nonverbal behaviors.

Teachers should be enthusiastic!

Maintain neatness in your teaching environment. A cluttered office, desk, classroom or work area may be perceived as reflections of your attitude. Nonverbally, you could communicate "I don't really care—why should you?"

Classroom environments influence student learning.

Still in its infancy, nonverbal research has been overshadowed by the popular attention given its older sibling, linguistic research. Connoisseurs of the subtleties of nonverbal behavior recognize the multi-dimensionality of nonverbal experiences and analyze these cues within the context of various settings. Increasing awareness of one's nonverbal behavior requires practice and patience. As one works to improve nonverbal actions, the goal should be to foster positive characteristics, mannerisms, actions, and habits as well as to overcome negative traits that depress an atmosphere for learning.

Awareness, practice, and patience are the keys to understanding nonverbal messages.

Look and listen to both verbal and nonverbal messages being sent by students. Listen to not only the words being said, but also to how the words are said. Look for communication cues such as students' posture, facial expressions, eye behavior, and body movements and gestures.

It is also very important that teachers pay attention to their own nonverbal behavior.

Teachers should be aware of students' posture and other nonverbal messages.

Specifically, monitor your external signs such as tone of voice, body position, and facial expressions in response to others. Being aware of your nonverbal signals will help you communicate more effectively.

To help teachers avoid any dogmatic evaluation of student nonverbal behaviors, a final point needs to be made. No formalized reliable means have been developed to identify and interpret all nonverbal behaviors. Many student nonverbal behaviors are autonomic, idiosyncratic, and ambiguous when considered out of context. Thus, it is important not to jump to conclusions or to make generalizations without considering three validity checks: (1) deviant behavior from a baseline, (2) cultural background, and (3) gender differences.

"I have learned to depend more on what people do than what they say in response to a direct question, to pay close attention to that which cannot be consciously manipulated, and to look for patterns rather than content."

Edward T. Hall

Teachers should notice when students exhibit uncharacteristic behavior.

The first validity check on nonverbal communication considers deviant behavior from a standard pattern. For instance, it is important to notice when a student is exhibiting uncharacteristic behavior. The critical point is not noticing the frequency of behavior but rather identifying the discrepancies.

The second validity check on nonverbal communication considers the individual's specific upbringing and culture. We learn a great deal of our nonverbal skills as a child in our formative years. At a very early age we learn how far to stand from another person, what type of physical touching is appropriate, and when and how long to make eye contact. These lessons are not formally taught, but learned from our cultural experiences.

Nonverbal behaviors and their perceptions are different for many cultures. The six classic nonverbal emotions that have the same meaning all over the world are happiness, sadness, anger, disgust, surprise, and fear.

People signal happiness by smiles, sadness by tears, and anger by raised voices or strong gestures. The ability to read or speak a foreign language does

Body language has different meanings in different cultures.

"To acquire knowledge, one must study; but to acquire wisdom, one must observe."

Marilyn vos Savant

Teachers' perceptions of nonverbal behaviors will vary for students from other cultures.

not guarantee an understanding of the cultural aspects that go beyond the verbal message. What is correct in one country may not be considered appropriate in another.

Teachers, administrators, and counselors must make personal adjustments to compensate for the cultural diversity found in classrooms. Obviously, cross-cultural differences found in Florida classrooms will not be the same as those found in New York classrooms. Those who teach or work in such culturally pluralistic situations need to acquire knowledge and empathy to interpret correctly the meaning of these nonverbal differences.

A recent study analyzed North American university students' perceptions of five nonverbal cues (voice, space, eyes, facial expressions, and hand gestures) in intercultural interviews of 103 individuals from Africa, Asia, Europe, Latin America, and the Middle East. The findings indicated that North American perceptions of nonverbal behaviors varied for each culture studied. (See Table 2).

"To effectively communicate, we must realize that we are all different in the way we perceive the world and use this understanding as a guide to our communication with others."

Anthony Robbins

"The older I grow the more I listen to people who don't talk much."

Germain G. Glien

TABLE 2
NORTH AMERICAN PERCEPTIONS OF NONVERBAL BEHAVIORS EXHIBITED IN SELECTED FOREIGN COUNTRIES

Country	Voice	Space	Eyes	Facial Expressions	Hand Gestures
African	Softer volume and slower rate	Closer distance	Less gaze	More smiling	No consensus
Asian	Softer volume and slower rate	Closer distance	Less eye contact and gaze	Less emotion and more smiling	Fewer and smaller in size
European	Softer volume and faster rate	Closer distance	More eye contact and gaze	Less emotion and more smiling	No consensus
Latin American	Softer volume and slower rate	Closer distance	Less eye contact and gaze	Less emotion and more smiling	Fewer and smaller in size
Middle Eastern	Faster rate	Closer distance	More eye contact	More emotion and more smiling	More expansive

Ostermeier, T. (1994). Differences in Meaning for Nonverbal Cues and Ease/Difficulty in Intercultural Listening.

The third validity check on nonverbal communication considers gender differences. Many nonverbal cues and behaviors can be misinterpreted because of boys' and girls' stereotyped upbringings. Treated differently from birth, boys and girls usually act differently. Research has shown that while males are believed to be more aggressive, athletic, and mechanical, females are thought to be more conforming, quiet, and generally interested in scholarly activities. Teachers may, however, notice in some girls an aggressiveness that can be related to increased participation in competitive sports. Moreover, it is not at all uncommon to find boys who are much

"As I grow older, I pay less attention to what men say. I just watch what they do."

Andrew Carnegie

Many nonverbal behaviors could be misinterpreted because of boys' and girls' stereotyped upbringings.

more interested in science or music than in sporting events.

Communication experts are finding that nonverbal messages are far more pervasive and relevant in the everyday world than generally realized.

Research has suggested that nonverbal messages may be used by a judge to influence a jury's decision, a physician to affect the course of a patient's treatment, a teacher to influence a student's intellectual progress, and a manager to control subordinates.

These messages, however, are more complex and subtle than some literature has suggested. Be aware, though, that much of the literature on nonverbal communication leaves the impression that all nonverbal cues (such as crossed legs and head nods) have implicit meanings. This impression is erroneous because the meanings depend on when and where the cues are exhibited. For example, yawning may indicate boredom in one situation or simply mean the person is tired in another situation. Not all body language is significant; in fact, no single nonverbal action conveys true meaning of a situation. Nonverbal behaviors may not have implicit meaning; they must be considered in context.

"You see, but you do not observe. The distinction is clear."

Sherlock Holmes to Watson in Sir Arthur Conan Doyle's book *A Scandal in Bohemia*

Although some nonverbal actions may be given more weight than others, oversimplifying the analysis of these behaviors should be avoided.

In order to succeed in today's classroom, teachers must have an understanding and command of body language. Your nonverbal communication will either strengthen or weaken your communication with others. Having the power to send positive nonverbal messages and not let negative nonverbal actions escape takes awareness and practice. Most top business people, lawyers, politicians, and salespeople practice in front of mirrors or record themselves in order to critique facial expressions, body movements, gestures, and overall presentation.

Nonverbal awareness implies a conscious effort to employ all the senses in receiving and sending messages. Insights into nonverbal communication not only heighten sensitivity to others, but inevitably strengthen self-understanding as well. Communication between teachers and students can be greatly improved by better understanding the use of body language. Just as teachers have spent a great deal of time and energy perfecting their teaching skills, they must also devote time and energy to developing nonverbal communication skills.

Self-awareness is critical to improving nonverbal communication.

"You can observe a lot just by watching."

Lawrence Peter ("Yogi") Berra

"Who dares to teach must never cease to learn."

John Cotton Dana

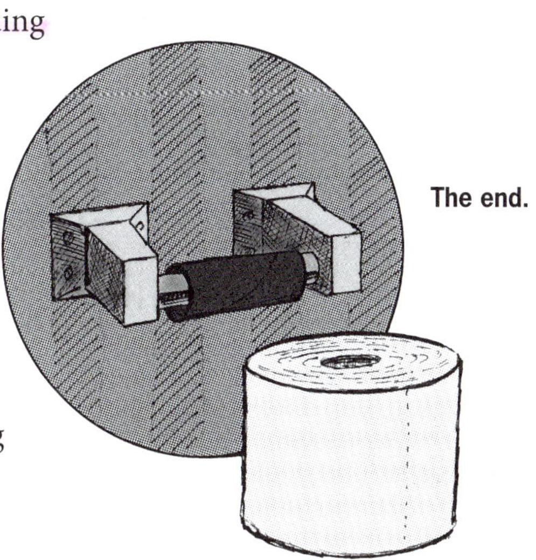

The end.

GUIDELINES

GENERAL	Yes	No
Are your verbal and nonverbal messages consistent?		
Do your nonverbal messages indicate a consistent treatment of students?		
Do your nonverbal messages encourage all students to participate in class activities?		
Do your nonverbal messages show that you expect all students can learn?		
Do your nonverbal messages project warmth and enthusiasm?		
Do your nonverbal actions project confidence, fairness, and friendliness?		
Do you provide positive nonverbal feedback to students?		
Do you provide neat and attractive instructional handouts?		
Do you consider cultural and gender differences before judging students?		

FACIAL EXPRESSIONS	Yes	No
Do your facial cues convey positive expressions when interacting with students?		
Do you smile to provide reassurance and approval?		
Are you aware of your facial expressions?		
Are you able to interpret students' facial expressions?		
Are you able to "read" students' faces when they need help?		

EYE BEHAVIOR	Yes	No
Do you make eye contact with all students?		
Do your eyes convey a message of caring?		
Do students look at you when you are talking?		
Can you tell when students don't understand the topic by looking at their eyes?		
Can you tell if students are bored with a topic or need a break by studying their eyes?		
Do you use a stern look to handle obvious cheaters in testing situations?		

TOUCHING	Yes	No
Do you pat students on the back or arm to congratulate them for performing well?		
Do you use a firm handshake when greeting parents or classroom guests?		

VOCAL INTONATION	Yes	No
Is your voice loud enough so all students can hear you?		
Do you vary tone and pitch to emphasize words?		
Does your voice project confidence?		
Can you tell when students are sincere by listening to their vocal qualities?		
Do you use your voice to reinforce student responses to questions?		
Do you pronounce students' names correctly?		
Do you speak at a moderate rate (not too slowly and not too rapidly)?		
Does your voice project enthusiasm for the subject matter being taught?		
Do you pause to encourage student contributions?		

BODY MOVEMENTS AND GESTURES	Yes	No
Are you aware of students' positive and negative body movements and gestures?		
Are you cognizant of students' posture in the classroom?		
Do you lean forward when listening to students' questions or comments?		
Are your gestures natural and consistent with your verbal messages?		
Do you stand up straight, without slouching, in the front of a class of students?		
Do your body movements and gestures communicate confidence and self-assurance?		
Do you use hand motions to provide direction to students?		

USE OF SPACE	Yes	No
Do you maintain a consistent space between you and all students?		
Do you maintain a neat and clean teaching environment?		
Do you use different travel routes in the classroom to interact with all students?		
Does the arrangement of classroom furniture allow for effective communication?		
Does your work space project a comfortable and welcome feeling?		

DRESS	Yes	No
Does your attire represent a professional image appropriate for your school?		
Do you wear clean and acceptable clothing?		
Do you wear suitable jewelry or accessories?		

REVIEW EXERCISE

Directions: For items 1-60, circle "T" for TRUE statements and "F" for FALSE statements. Answers are found on page 92.

Introduction/Research

T F 1. Communication is composed of verbal and nonverbal messages.

T F 2. Research findings suggest that two-thirds of our communication is nonverbal.

T F 3. Validity and reliability of verbal messages are checked by nonverbal actions.

T F 4. The left hemisphere of the brain is responsible for nonverbal processes.

T F 5. Nonverbal behavior tells other people what we expect of them.

T F 6. Educators, psychologists, anthropologists, and sociologists define nonverbal communication as communication without words.

T F 7. Nonverbal messages are more authentic than spoken words.

T F 8. Nonverbal behaviors can support or contradict verbal messages.

Facial Expressions

T F 9. Muscle movements that cause changes in the forehead, eyebrows, eyelids, cheeks, nose, lips, and chin register facial expressions.

T F 10. Some facial expressions are readily visible; while other facial expressions are so fleeting they go unnoticed.

T F 11. Facial expressions are the primary source of information next to words in determining an individual's internal feelings.

T F 12. The face is capable of producing 20,000 different expressions.

T F 13. Fear causes voluntary facial expressions.

T F 14. People of all cultures display different facial cues for emotions such as happiness and fear.

Eye Behavior

T F 15. Eye behavior can regulate human interaction.

T F 16. Eyes can send and receive messages.

T F 17. People tend to look longer and more often at those whom they trust.

T F 18. People control normal eye dilation.

T F 19. When looking at something pleasing, an individual's pupils will constrict.

T F 20. Eye contact can be manipulated to open or close channels of communication.

T F 21. Direct eye contact can express support or disapproval.

Vocal Intonation

T F 22. Vocal intonation is the most understood and valid area of nonverbal communication.

T F 23. Despair is vocalized by high pitch and words uttered quickly.

T F 24. If verbal information contradicts vocal intonation, verbal will dominate.

T F 25. Vocal intonation reveals emotional conditions.

T F 26. Words can have different meanings depending on how they are said.

Touching

T F 27. Tactual sensitivity begins during childhood and greatly contributes to the mental and emotional adjustment of an individual.

T F 28. At adolescence little touching occurs between parents and children beyond hands and arms.

T F 29. Touching between adults in the United States is taboo except under certain socially accepted conditions.

T F 30. The right to touch someone in our society is determined by status.

T F 31. Touching in the classroom is a delicate matter.

T F 32. Touching, such as a "pat on the back," can be used as a positive reinforcer in the classroom.

Body Movements and Gestures

T F 33. People communicate by the way they walk, stand, and sit.

T F 34. Crime prevention experts tell us that muggers look for victims that exhibit alert body movements and postures.

T F 35. Postural relaxation can denote status or strength in a relationship.

T F 36. Speech is comprehended quicker than gestures.

T F 37. Body posture can be accurately observed from a distance.

T F 38. People in the United States have a narrow postural vocabulary and have a difficult time accepting postural ranges found in other countries.

T F 39. Body movements are frequent indicators of status.

Use of Space

T F 40. "Kinesics" indicates territory to which access is allowed or denied to other people or objects.

T F 41. Informal space refers to the personal distance around individuals.

T F 42. Semi-fixed-feature space refers to immovable walls or partitions and objects.

T F 43. Physical environment can create moods and establish how much communication takes place.

T F 44. Physical arrangement of furniture can dictate spatial boundaries.

T F 45. Classroom environment affects students' attitudes.

T F 46. Clutter in the work environment is an indication of a busy teacher.

T F 47. In straight-row seating, interaction is greatest in the front and middle rows, whether seating is imposed or self-selected.

T F 48. Our personal space changes size and shape depending on the situation.

T F 49. In the United States, a 5- to 12-foot distance is acceptable for interaction between friends.

T **F** 50. Adults in the United States accept physical closeness only for intimate relationships.

T **F** 51. Most people stand farther away from those with disabilities, those from different racial backgrounds, and authority figures.

Dress

T **F** 52. Dress can indicate group membership or time in history.

T **F** 53. Appropriate dress is a method of expressing respect for both the particular situation and the people in it.

T **F** 54. Dress can alienate or persuade others.

T **F** 55. Clunky jewelry, garish makeup, and strong cologne speak volumes without saying a word.

Final Comments

T **F** 56. To be an effective communicator, nonverbal behaviors must be learned and practiced.

T **F** 57. Formalized reliable means have been developed to identify and interpret nonverbal behaviors.

T **F** 58. Nonverbal behaviors are ambiguous when considered out of context.

T **F** 59. One should consider gender differences before analyzing nonverbal behaviors.

T **F** 60. Teachers should avoid oversimplifying the analysis of nonverbal behaviors.

BIBLIOGRAPHY

Adams, S. (2003). *When body language goes bad: A Dilbert book.* Kansas City, MO: Andrews McMeel Publishing.

Akhtar, S. & Kramer, S., (Ed.). (1992). *When the body speaks: Psychological meaning in kinetic clues.* Northvale, NJ: Aronson.

Ambady, N. (2004). *Interpersonal perceptions and communication laboratory.* Cambridge, MA: Harvard University.

Andersen, P.A. (1998). *Nonverbal communication: Forms and functions.* New York: McGraw-Hill.

Axctell, R. (1997). *Gestures: The do's and taboos of body language around the world.* New York: John Wiley & Sons.

Baringer, D.K. & McCroskey, J.C. (2000). Immediacy in the classroom: Student immediacy. *Communication Education,* 49(2), 178-186.

Baum, N. (1994). Learn to be a good communicator and a good listener. *American Medical News,* 37(14), 34.

Bonniwell-Haslett, B. & Samter, W. (1997). *Children communicating the first five years.* Mahwah, NJ: Lawrence Erbaum Associates.

Boothman, N. (2000). *How to make people like you in 90 seconds or less.* New York: Workman Publishing.

Cahn, D.D. (1986). The role of perceived understanding in supervisor-subordinate communication and organizational effectiveness. *Central States Speech Journal,* 37(1), 19-26.

Chamberlin, C.R. (2000). Nonverbal behaviors and initial impressions of trustworthiness in teacher-supervisor relationships. *Communication Education,* 49(4), 352-363.

Cooper, H. & Good, T. (1983). *Pygmalion grows up: Studies in expectation communication process.* New York: Longman.

Davitz, J. R. (1976). *The communication of emotional meaning.* New York: McGraw-Hill.

Dimitrius, J. & Mazzarella, M. (1998). *Reading people.* New York: Random House.

Doherty-Sneddon, G. (2003). *Children's unspoken language.* New York: Jessica Kingsley Publishers.

Duggan, A. P. & Rarrott, R. L. (2001). Physicians' nonverbal rapport building and patients' talk about the subjective component of illness. *Human Communication Research,* 27(2), 299-311.

Ekman, P. (2003). *Emotions revealed: Recognizing faces and feelings to improve communication and emotional life.* New York: Times Books.

Ekman, P. (2001). *Telling lies: Clues to deceit in the marketplace, politics, and marriage.* New York: W.W. Norton & Company.

Ekman, P. & Rosenberg, E. (1998). *What the face reveals: Basic and applied studies of spontaneous expression using the facial action coding system.* New York: Oxford University Press.

Elksnin, L.K. & Elksnin, N. (2000). Teaching parents to teach their children to be prosocial. *Intervention in School & Clinic,* 36(1), 27-35.

Emerson, R.W. (1873). *The prose works of Ralph Waldo Emerson (Volume. 2).* Boston: James R. Osgood.

Fast, J. (1994). *Body language in the workplace.* New York: Penguin Group.

Feldman, R.S. (Ed.). (1992). *Applications of nonverbal behavior theories and research.* Hillsdale, NJ: L. Erlbaum Associates.

Fisher-Griggs, L. (2001). Do students behave better when the teacher is well dressed? *NEA Today,* 20(3), 20.

Freud, S. (1901). *The psychopathology of everyday life.* New York: W.W. Norton.

Galloway, C. M. (1972). The challenge of nonverbal communication. *Theory into Practice,* 10(4), 227-230.

Givens, D. B. (2001). *The nonverbal dictionary of gestures, signs and body language cues.* Spokane, WA: Center for Nonverbal Studies Press.

Glass, L. (2002). *I know what you're thinking: Using the four codes of reading people to improve your life.* New York: John Wiley & Sons.

Gladwell, M. (2005). *Blink: The power of thinking without thinking.* New York: Time Warner.

Goldin-Meadow, S. & Singer, M.A. (2003). From children's hands to adult's ears: Gesture's role in teaching and learning. *Developmental Psychology, 39,* 509-520.

Gorham, J., Cohen, S.H. & Morris T.L. (1999). Fashion in the classroom III: Effects of instructor attire and immediacy in natural classroom interactions. *Communication Quarterly,* 47(3), 281-300.

Greffin, M.A. & McGhee, D. (1995). Watch what you're saying when you're not talking. *School Business Affairs,* 61(1), 46-49.

Grifin, J. & Power, T. (1998). *How to say it at work: Putting yourself across with power words, phases, body language, and communication secrets.* Upper Saddle River, NJ: Prentice Hall.

Guerrero, L.K., Devito, J.A. & Hecht, M. L. (1999). *The nonverbal communication reader: Classic and contemporary readings.* Long Grove, IL: Waveland Press.

Hall, E.T. (1969). *The hidden dimension.* Garden City, NY: Doubleday.

Hartley, M. (2003). *Body language at work.* London: Sheldon Press.

Hickson, M.L., Stacks, D.W. & Moore, N. (2004). *Nonverbal communication: Studies and applications (4th ed.).* Los Angeles, CA: Roxbury Publishing.

Hinton, B.E. (1985). Selected nonverbal communication factors influencing adult behavior and learning. *Lifelong Learning,* 8(8), 23-26.

Holinger, P. (2003). *What babies say before they can talk: The nine signals infants use to express their feelings.* New York: Fireside.

Hugenberg, K., & Bodenhausen, G. V. (2004). Ambiguity in social categorization: The role of prejudice and facial affect in race categorization. *Psychological Science, 15,* 342-345.

Joseph, R. (2000). The evolution of sex differences in language, sexuality, and visual-spatial skills. *Archives of Sexual Behavior,* 29(1), 35-67.

Knapp, M.L. & Hall, J.A. (1992). *Nonverbal communication in human interaction (3rd ed.).* Forth Worth: Harcourt Brace.

Kolaric, G.C. & Galambos, N.L. (1995). Face-to-face interactions in unacquainted female-male dyads: How do girls and boys behave? *Journal of Early Adolescence,* 15(3), 363-382.

Kuzdzal, S.J. (1981). Interaction of student cognitive and psychomotor characteristics with vocational teachers' nonverbal communication behaviors. Doctoral dissertation, Wayne State University, 1981. *Dissertation Abstracts International,* 42, 4808A.

Krannich, C. & Krannich, R. (2000). *Savvy interviewing: The nonverbal advantage.* Manassas Park, Virginia: Impact Publications.

Leathers, D.G. (1986). *Successful nonverbal communication: Principles and applications.* New York: Macmillan.

Leeds, D. (1995). Body language: Actions speak louder than words. *National Underwriter Life and Health-Financial Services Edition,* 18(1), 18-20.

Levine, D. & Adelman, M. (1993). *Beyond language: Cross-cultural communication.* Englewood Cliffs, NJ: Regents/Prentice-Hall.

Malandro, L.A., Barker, L.L. & Barker, D.A. (1989). *Nonverbal communication (2nd ed.).* New York: Random House.

Marlow, L., Bloss, K. & Bloss, D. (2000). Promoting social and emotional competency through teacher/counselor collaboration. *Education,* 120(4), 668-675.

Martin, B. & Newcomer, S. (2002). A descriptive study of gender equity in rural secondary classroom situations. *Rural Educator,* 23(3), 37-46.

Martin, S. (1995). The role of nonverbal communications in quality improvement. *National Productivity Review,* 15(1), 27-40.

McCormick, T.E. & Noriega, T. (1986). Low versus high expectations: A review of teacher expectations' effects on minority students. *Journal of Educational Equity and Leadership,* 6(3), 224-34.

McCoy, L. (1996). First impressions. *Canadian Banker,* 103(5), 32-36.

McGinty, K., Knox, D. & Zusman, M.E. (2003). Nonverbal and verbal communication in "involved" and "casual" relationships among college students. *College Student Journal,* 37(1), 68-72.

McNeilis, K.S. (2002). Assessing communication competence in the primary care medical interview. *Communication Studies,* 53(4), 401-430.

Mehrabian, A. (1968). Communication without words. *Psychology Today,* 2, 53-55.

Miller, P.W. (2000). *Nonverbal communication in the classroom.* Munster, IN: Patrick W. Miller and Associates.

Molnar, P. & Segerstrale, U., (Ed.). (1997). *Nonverbal communication: Where nature meets culture.* Mahwah, NJ: Lawrence Erlbaum Associates.

Nelson, A. & Golant, S.K. (2004). *You don't say: Navigating nonverbal communication between the sexes.* Upper Saddle River, NJ: Prentice Hall.

Nierenberg, G.I. & Calero, H.H. (1993). *How to read a person like a book.* New York: Barnes & Noble.

Nolen, W.E. (1995). Reading people. *Internal Auditor,* 52(2), 48-52.

Ostermeier, T. (1994). Differences in meaning for nonverbal cues and ease/difficulty in intercultural listening. *Paper presented at the Annual Meeting of the International Listening Association Convention,* Boston, MA.

Pearson, J.C. (1985). *Gender and communication.* Dubuque, IA: William C. Brown.

Quilliam, S. (1995). *Body language: How to understand and master the use of bodytalk in the workplace, at home, and in social situations.* New York: Crescent Books.

Ramsey, R.D. (2002). *How to say the right thing every time: Communicating well with students, staff, parents, and the public.* Thousand Oaks, CA: Corwin.

Remland, M.S. (2004). *Nonverbal communication in everyday life (2nd ed.).* Boston: Houghton Mifflin.

Ribbens, G. & Thompson, R. (2001). *Understanding body language.* Hauppauge, NY: Barrons Educational Series.

Richmond, V.P. & McCroskey, J.C. (2003). *Nonverbal behavior in interpersonal relations (5th ed.).* Boston: Pearson, Allyn & Bacon.

Rosenthal, R. & Jacobsen, L. (1968). *Pygmalion in the classroom.* New York: Holt, Rinehart and Winston.

Russell, A. (1992). Fine-tuning your corporate image. *Black Enterprise,* 22(10), 72-84.

Schwebel, D.C. & Schwebel, M. (2002). Teaching nonverbal communication. *College Teaching,* 50(3), 88-92.

Schopenhauer, A. (1891). In Saunders T. Bailey, Trans. *"On physiognomy." Religion: A dialogue and other essays.* New York: Macmillian, 75-85.

Shapiro, L.E. (2003). *The Secret language of children: How to understand what your kids are really saying.* Naperville, IL: Sourcebooks Trade.

Sheldrick Ross, C. & Dewdney, P. (1998). *Communicating professionally.* New York: Neal-Schuman Publishers, Inc.

Skelly, F.J. (1992). Communicating care. *American Medical News,* 35(13), 39-44.

Spangler, L. (1995). Gender-specific nonverbal communication: Impact for speaker effectiveness. *Human Resource Development Quarterly,* 6(4), 409-419.

Steele, R.D. (1999). *Body language secrets: A guide during courtship and dating.* Whitter, CA: Steel Balls Press.

Sternberg, R. (2003). Attending to teacher attire. *School Administrator,* 60(2), 38-42; 44; 46.

Swenson, J. & Casmir, F. L. (1998). The impact of culture-sameness, gender, foreign travel, and academic background on the ability to interpret facial expression of emotion in others. *Communication Quarterly,* 46(2), 214-231.

Trees, A.R. (2000). Nonverbal communication and the support process: Interactional sensitivity in interactions between mothers and young adult children. *Communications Monographs,* 67(3), 239-261.

Thomas, D.L. (1996). The self-fulfilling prophecy: Better management through magic. *Trusts and Estates,* 135(11), 20-22.

Timm, S. & Schroeder, B.L. (2000). Listening/nonverbal communication training. *International Journal of Listening,* 14, 109-128.

Valenzeno, L., Alibali, M.W. & Klatzky, R. (2003). Teachers' gestures facilitate students' learning: A lesson in symmetry. *Contemporary Educational Psychology, 28,* 187-204.

Vargas, M.F. (1986). *Louder than words: An introduction to nonverbal communication.* Ames, IA: Iowa State University Press.

Waggoner, C. (2002). Blue denim blues. *School Administrator,* 59(2), 66.

Wainright, G.R. (1999). *Body language.* Lincolnwood, IL: Contemporary Publishing.

Wainright, G.R. (2003). *Teach yourself body language.* New York: McGraw-Hill.

Wiest, L. (1999). Practicing what they teach; should teachers do as they say? *Clearing House,* 72(5), 264.

Williams, J.W. & Eggland, S.A. (1985). *Communication in action.* Cincinnati, OH: Southwestern.

Woolfolk, A.E. & Galloway, C.M. (1985). Nonverbal communication and the study of teaching. *Theory into Practice,* 24(1), 77-84.

INDEX

Subjects

Authors Quoted

Review Exercise Answers

1. True	11. True	21. True	31. True	41. True	51. True
2. True	12. True	22. True	32. True	42. False	52. True
3. True	13. False	23. False	33. True	43. True	53. True
4. False	14. False	24. False	34. False	44. True	54. True
5. True	15. True	25. True	35. True	45. True	55. True
6. True	16. True	26. True	36. False	46. False	56. True
7. True	17. True	27. True	37. True	47. True	57. False
8. True	18. False	28. True	38. True	48. True	58. True
9. True	19. False	29. True	39. True	49. False	59. True
10. True	20. True	30. True	40. False	50. True	60. True